THE
SHELTER
OF
GOD'S PROMISES

Ps. 1 ~

I Cr ♡ 2.1 a

Gary Miracle

y SHEILA WALSH

...an Trusts God
...Pray
...our Life

...hat Really Matters
Extraordinary Faith
I'm Not Wonder Woman but God Made Me Wonderful
A Love So Big
Living Fearlessly
Stories from the River of Mercy
Stones from the River of Mercy
The Heartache No One Sees
Life Is Tough but God Is Faithful
Gifts for Your Soul
Honestly
Bring Back the Joy
Best Devotions of Sheila Walsh
Sparks in the Dark

FICTION

Angel Song (with Kathryn Cushman)

CHILDREN'S BOOKS

Hello, Sun!
Hello, Stars!

God's Little Princess series:
Sweet Dreams Princess
I Am Loved
God's Little Princess Bible
A God's Little Princess Treasury (Gigi)
The Pink Ballerina (Gigi)
The Purple Ponies (Gigi)
The Perfect Christmas Gift (Gigi)
The Royal Tea Party (Gigi)
There's a Princess in Me (Gigi)
Gigi, God's Little Princess

God's Mighty Warrior series:
Goodnight Warrior
I Am Amazing
Will, God's Mighty Warrior
The Creepy Caves Mystery
The Mystery of Magillicuddy's Gold
God's Mighty Warrior Devotional Bible

The Gnoo Zoo series:
In Search of the Great White Tiger
Chattaboonga's Chilling Choice
Miss Marbles's Marvelous Makeover
Einstein's Enormous Error
Big Billy's Great Adventure

GIFT BOOKS

God's Shelter in Your Storm
Outrageous Love
Come As You Are
Good Morning, Lord

COAUTHORED WOMEN OF FAITH BOOKS

Women of Faith Devotional Bible
Discovering God's Will for Your Life
The Great Adventure
Irrepressible Hope
Sensational Life
Time to Rejoice
Nothing Is Impossible
A Grand New Day
Infinite Grace
Contagious Joy
Laugh Out Loud
Amazing Freedom
The Women of Faith Daily Devotional
The Women of Faith Study Guide Series

THE
SHELTER
OF
GOD'S PROMISES

SHEILA WALSH

THOMAS NELSON
Since 1798

NASHVILLE DALLAS MEXICO CITY RIO DE JANEIRO

The Shelter of God's Promises

© 2011 by Sheila Walsh

All rights reserved. No portion of this book may be reproduced, stored in a retrieval system, or transmitted in any form or by any means—electronic, mechanical, photocopy, recording, or any other—except for brief quotation in printed reviews, without the prior written permission of the publisher.

Published in Nashville, Tennessee. Thomas Nelson is a registered trademark of Thomas Nelson, Inc.

Thomas Nelson, Inc. titles may be purchased in bulk for educational, business, fund-raising, or sales promotional use. For information, please e-mail SpecialMarkets@ThomasNelson.com.

All Scripture quotations are taken from HOLY BIBLE: NEW INTERNATIONAL VERSION®. © 1973, 1978, 1984 by International Bible Society. Used by permission of Zondervan Publishing House. All rights reserved.

Man of the Tombs © 1989 Matters of the Heart Music (ASCAP). Words and music by Bob Bennett www.bobbennett.com.

ISBN 978-1-4002-8110-7 (hard cover)

The Library of Congress has catalogued the trade paper edition as follows:

Walsh, Sheila, 1956–
    The shelter of God's promises / Sheila Walsh.
        p. cm.
    Includes bibliographical references (p.).
    ISBN 978-1-4002-0244-7
    1. Christian women—Religious life. 2. God (Christianity)—Promises.
I. Title.
BV4527.W356 2011
248.8'43—dc22
                                    2010042293

Printed in the United States of America

HB 09.09.2020

This book is dedicated to one of my most treasured friends, Ney Bailey. I will be eternally grateful for the multitude of ways that your life is a radiant reminder of the promises of Christ to me.

CONTENTS

Acknowledgments   ix

Introduction: In the Cleft of the Rock / A Night Alone in the Storm   xi

 1. Promises, Promises / *I Need Something to Hold On To*   1

 2. Provision / *I Don't Have Enough*   19

 3. Peace / *I'm Afraid and Feel Alone*   41

 4. Confidence / *I Can't See God's Plan in This Pain*   57

 5. Love / *I Don't Believe That Anyone Could Really Love Me*   77

 6. Grace / *I Have Failed*   97

 7. Hope / *I'm Broken*   117

 8. Strength / *I Feel Things Are Crashing Around Me*   133

 9. More / *I Know There's Something Better*   149

10. Home / *I Have a Future*   165

Notes   187

Bible Study   191

About the Author   205

ACKNOWLEDGMENTS

I am deeply grateful to the team that worked with me on this life-changing journey through the Word of God:

Brian Hampton, thank you for your leadership and vision.

Bryan Norman, you always give so much more than is asked, but this time you circled the earth twice! Thank you, Bryan.

Jeanette Thomason, thank you for pouring yourself wholeheartedly into this project.

Jennifer Stair, your careful attention to detail is such a gift.

Michael Hyatt and the entire team at Thomas Nelson, it is a privilege to be in such creative company.

Mary Graham and the Women of Faith family, thank you from the bottom of my heart for the platform to be able to share with thousands of women across the country about the love and grace of God.

Barry Walsh, I am so grateful to you for your heart for this book. You helped me every step of the way, and the finished project is so much stronger because of you. Thank you!

My deepest gratitude is to You, Lord Jesus Christ. Thank You that we can stake our lives on Your promises and find shelter for our lives in You.

Introduction

IN THE CLEFT
OF THE ROCK

A Night Alone in the Storm

Then the LORD said, "There is a place near me where you may stand on a rock. When my glory passes by, I will put you in a cleft in the rock and cover you with my hand until I have passed by."

—EXODUS 33:21–22

Whether it's the Ritz Carlton or a Motel 6, every traveler knows the importance of finding shelter by night—a place to rest, to claim refuge from the day, and to greet the dawn's promise and splendor of a new morning.

Even at age eighteen, I knew this.

So when my high school friends Linda and Moira and I boarded a train from our home in Ayr, on the west coast of Scotland, we carted an impressive collection of sleeping bags, backpacks, and tent gear for our all-girls camping trip. If you are thinking Girl Scouts, think more *Beverly Hillbillies*. Shelter would be on our minds by evening. First, we would change trains at Glasgow, with our destination Aviemore, the very center of Cairngorms National Park.

The Cairngorms, in the eastern Highlands of Scotland, consist of five of Scotland's tallest mountains, each beautiful and remote. They promised adventure, and I was excited to explore, hoping to spot a golden eagle or a snowy owl.

How I loved the idea of being an explorer. Growing up on the west coast of Scotland, I admired men and women who set off into the unknown, particularly those who lived to tell their stories. Seeing the craggy and wild Cairngorms, still ridged with ripples of snow, I thought, *This won't be easy, this living to tell the tale.* Living remained a tad more appealing though.

Linda, Moira, and I set off from the train, then, to trek into all-new territory. We decided to go easy that first night, hiking just three miles into the mountain range. The wildness of the place gave an ominous, unspoken warning that we should pitch our tents while there was enough daylight. Even from the train platform, we'd been awed by the long-extended plateaus of Braeriach and the great massive slopes of the Cairngorm Mountains. Now, as we headed into and up the mountain, we were surrounded on all sides by shafts of sunlight intermittent with writhing mists and deep shadows in clefts shining and silvery with remnants of snow. Inner recesses revealed bleak cliffs, red granite slopes, and the rugged jaws of the mountain.

Before ascending, we found what looked to be a good place for tenting that night, then lit a small fire to boil some water—because even in the wild, we Scots need our tea. Before settling into our individual tents, I wanted to celebrate the beautiful night. I climbed to the highest vantage point to watch the sun set behind the mountains.

Then I climbed back down to crawl into my sleeping bag, turned on my flashlight, and read one of my favorite psalms. Called a "song of ascents," Psalm 121 seemed so very fitting:

> *I lift up my eyes to the hills—*
>> *where does my help come from?*
> *My help comes from the LORD,*
>> *the Maker of heaven and earth.*
>
> *He will not let your foot slip—*
>> *he who watches over you will not slumber;*
> *indeed, he who watches over Israel*
>> *will neither slumber nor sleep.*
>
> *The LORD watches over you—*
>> *the LORD is your shade at your right hand;*
> *the sun will not harm you by day,*
>> *nor the moon by night.*
>
> *The LORD will keep you from all harm—*
>> *he will watch over your life;*
> *the LORD will watch over your coming and going*
>> *both now and forevermore.*

In the wild, strange sounds swirl all about you from the deepest darkness you can imagine: birds settling down for the night, the crackle of tree branches in mountain breezes, the rustle of grass with the passing of unseen creepy beasts that I was afraid had made reservations in my sleeping bag for the night. Still, Psalm 121 comforted me, and I drifted into a deep, peaceful sleep, the picture of this beautiful place clear in my mind's eye.

When I woke, I was cold and it was drizzly outside. Drizzle is the name we give a certain kind of rain in Scotland. It's not substantial enough to be a decent rainfall but still manages to get you soaking wet. So I changed into warmer clothes for the day as Moira heated a can of baked beans and cooked sausages on sticks over the fire pit. I fetched some water from a stream to make tea, and we ate while looking over our map. Once we settled on where we were and where we wanted to be by sunset, we began packing up and set off on our first full day of expedition.

The hike was demanding that day, and not just because of the drizzle. The wind blew straight into our faces. At times, we couldn't see where to go. By sunset, however, we managed to log in ten miles and knew we needed to find shelter from the wind to pitch our tents.

Once I had my tent truly anchored, I tried to light a fire, and so did the others.

Tried was as far as any of us got. The wind blew and blew, and at times it sounded like a wolf howling in the mountains. Sitting in the dark and cold, the gusts pushing about us, I reminded God about His "not slumbering or sleeping and watching over me" promise. Then, seeing that there was nothing else to do, Linda, Moira, and I decided we should try to evade the storm by turning in for an early night's rest. I pulled two sweaters over my sweats and burrowed deep down into my sleeping bag. I listened to the wind blowing for a while before falling, once again, into a deep sleep.

The next thing I knew, I was wakened to the night in a state of confusion. At first I couldn't remember where I was, and, more pressing, something heavy was sitting on me. I could hardly breathe. I felt around in the dark for my flashlight and turned its beam onto the roof of my small tent. Something outside was flattening the tent and me, and I was terrified. I tried to call for Moira or Linda to help, but the wind was so loud, and I felt muffled by the weight on my face and chest. I thrashed my knees from my sleeping bag and pushed away from the tent wall until I managed to get out from underneath the pressure. Then I crawled out of the tent to see what on earth caused all this.

I almost jumped out of my Wellington boots when I came face-to-face with a rather large Scottish Highland sheep! I don't know which of us was more surprised, but the sheep made peace with the situation faster than I did and was clearly at rest for the night with no intention of getting up. I'm still not sure whether it had tried to lean against my tent for a wee nap or if it blew over, so I made one unsuccessful attempt to move its woolly self off my tent, and there was no point in waking Moira or Linda. There was no room in either of their tents for another body.

What to do? I didn't think it wise to join the sheep in the lean-to, so I pulled my sleeping bag out of the tent and tried to come up with a plan. The real problem was the wind. I knew I couldn't sleep completely exposed to the elements. But I remembered seeing a cave cut into the side of the mountain when we were scoping out the terrain. Using my flashlight, I made my way back to that cave. After making sure that I wasn't joining anything that might see me as a late-night snack, I crawled inside.

I made myself as comfortable as I could with my sleeping bag and settled in for the rest of the night. Although the wind kept howling outside, the cave was cut in such a way that I was completely sheltered. It was the unlikeliest of places, but when it seemed I was at my most displaced and exposed, I found myself more comfortable than ever.

Within no time, once again I was fast asleep.

The next morning, a brilliant light trickled into the cave where I slept. I crawled from my sleeping bag to see the sun rising, golden and bright, over the blue and purple silhouettes of the mountains. The calm and light, stillness and majesty surprised me after the gales of the night's storm. I felt as if God were saying, *Good morning, Sheila. Did you rest well? I kept you in the cleft just for this, just for the two of us to enjoy this together.*

I remember feeling at peace and loved, safe and protected and spared.

And then I heard my friends calling for me in panic and confusion. I was quickly dragged from the one-of-a-kind gift, the unfurling of the morning's splendor just for me. Instead, I was trying to explain to Moira and Linda that their friend and traveling companion had not transformed into Big Bertha, the mountain sheep.

We eventually completed our expedition, and we learned a lot about the value of a hefty sweater and ample amounts of hot tea. But now, Aviemore reminds me we are each travelers through this world. We're headed somewhere every day, as my friends and I were on those trains to the Cairngorm Mountains. Sometimes we have the adventurer's spirit to explore, to see how far we can get, how high we can climb. Sometimes we must change trains. Sometimes the rail we ride gets off track. There are accidents. Life happens. We tread into that unknown, fearful. We get tired and weary, confused, and sometimes wander. We lose our way. The weight of life presses down. Storms come. You don't get that job you counted on. The man you love doesn't love you back or share life as intimately as you desire. Your children, as much as you adore them, take a path you would never have chosen for them. A friend isn't there when you need her most. The bills keep coming, and you don't know how you're going to pay them. Your health fails. Someone you love dies. You want to accomplish great things, but you don't know how or where to start. You dream big dreams, but you can't seem to bring them to life or make them real. Or maybe things seem comfortable, yet you yearn for so much more—that mountaintop, a sunrise.

Where is your song of ascents? Where is the shelter God promised in Psalm 121, His help, His watchful eye on your comings and goings, His keeping of you from harm?

I think on this mystery often and of the cave outside Aviemore that gave me shelter from the storm, from the rain-ruled, dark night. What has had the most lasting impact on me is that, in the storm and under pressure, God took me to a place of rest, comfort, and ultimately, to a place of absolute beauty. Even among discomfort, disappointment, and displacement, I was kept safe. And from a cleft in the rock, a new day dawned, a glimpse of splendor and glory, and a moment of such beautiful fellowship with God that I knew He loved me deeply, intimately, surely, as sure as the rock I stood upon.

In the storm and under pressure, God took me to a place of rest, comfort, and ultimately, to a place of absolute beauty.

Promise maker
  "   Keeper

Promise give hope
even on your worse day his promises are
true.
          Viewing 3-7
March
5th Darlene - heart & exhaustion

   Judy - sister anxiety

   Kathy
   Mary - infection - trip to Pa.
                  tumors
   Grace friend (cancer Reyna)
   Bob Kirtland - blades removed
                           Cancer
   Shirley

1

PROMISES, PROMISES

I Need Something to Hold On To

THE PROMISE

*For no matter how many promises God has made, they are
"Yes" in Christ. And so through him the "Amen" is spoken
by us to the glory of God.*

—2 CORINTHIANS 1:20

When you think of promises, you don't want to think of what's
broken, of brokenness. It's human nature to want a sure thing
and for someone to back up the certainties, guaranteed, no questions
asked. But it's just like God to think of the unthinkable, to show us
that the impossible is possible, that there is one kind of brokenness
that holds everything together and in which promises are kept.

But I am jumping ahead of myself.

For me, choosing to study the promises of God in depth began with

1

a letter. I get very few actual delivered-to-my-mailbox letters these days. Most of my friends communicate via e-mail or text message, so a handwritten envelope on my desk was something of a novelty. I picked it up and tore at its seams with curiosity. Then I began to read.

I have never met the woman who wrote to me, but apparently she heard me speak at an event and sensed a connection with me. She wrote about some of the struggles she had been through in the past few years. These were not small things: illness, financial hardship, and the breakup of her marriage. Amid all these hardships, one line arrested my attention because of its profound simplicity:

"I would not have made it this far without the promises of God."

"I would not have made it this far
without the promises of God."

I read her letter again. On one hand, there was enormous human pain. On the other, words on paper from a God we can't see and the invisible help of the Holy Spirit. To some, the scales might have seemed imbalanced; the tangible hardships of her life left her body, heart, and soul stripped bare. Yet her confidence was compelling—beautifully and almost heartbreakingly compelling. Her words didn't read like wishful thinking but as a proclamation that has been lived out in an *I know that I know*, tear-bathed way.

I thought of friends and others I've met in my thirty years of speaking to women around the world. I remembered people who have faced similar, difficult circumstances and struggled to find hope in the middle of their messes. I've read through notes left on my Facebook page, notes slipped into my hand at the end of a speaking event. From the darkened caves of countless hearts, I have heard the same primal cry, the same questions over and again:

Has God forgotten me?

Does my life matter?

Is there a plan somewhere in all of this mess?

How am I going to make it?

How do I know God cares about my family?

What will happen to me when I die?

Will I die alone?

What if I outlive my children?

Why won't God heal my depression?

Why hasn't God healed my marriage?

How do I know that God even heard my prayer?

We want to believe that God sees everything, our comings and our goings, our slumber and our days, as Psalm 121 says. And we desperately need to know and feel that His promises hold true in the darkest of nights. We believe that God loves us, but bad things happen anyway. There are aftereffects and consequences, damage and wounds—pain that runs so deep that its presence, a reminder of the storms, invades our lives over and over.

The failures, disappointments, and regrets keep us questioning: Do God's promises hold fast when everything else is falling apart? What exactly does He promise us? Can we trust Him to keep His promises?

The failures, disappointments, and regrets keep us questioning: Do God's promises hold fast when everything else is falling apart?

THE PROMISE FOR KEEPS

Our deep, soul-level need for a "yes" to those questions hit home for me during the time my father-in-law, William, lived with us. Although we never verbalized it, my husband, Barry, and I assumed his mom would outlive his dad since William was twelve years older than Eleanor.

That's not what happened. Eleanor was diagnosed at sixty-seven with cancer, and she lived just two more years.

I have a vivid picture in my mind of William on the day of her funeral. Barry had taken our son, Christian, to the car, and William asked for a few minutes alone at the grave site after everyone else had left. I sat down under a tree covered in moss, its leaf-covered branches spreading in every direction like a divinely designed umbrella. I wanted to rest a moment and savor not only the peace there, the quiet, but the beauty after the hard-hitting emotions and unmooring of death and uncertainty in previous weeks. When I looked up, William was standing in his dark suit, silver hair all in place, hands crossed in front of him, like a little boy who was lost and didn't know what to do next.

We settled it that day: William would move from his home in Charleston, South Carolina, to live with us in Nashville, Tennessee.

"What if you get tired of me being here?" he asked one morning at breakfast.

"Pop, we're not going to get tired of you," I said. "You belong here. We were a family of three. Now we are a family of four."

"What are the house rules?" he asked.

"Oh, we have a very long list," I said with a smile. "Be kind to each other, and if you fall down, roll over, laugh a lot, and get back up."

Barry, Christian, and I loved having William in our home. He was funny and sweet and a great cook. His okra soup became a thing of legend! We were so glad that we could watch over him and simply enjoy him. Then one day something happened that caused him to—mentally, at least—pack his suitcases. We were discussing something at dinner. I don't even remember what it was now, but whatever I was saying, William disagreed with me and said so. I was a little surprised by the edge in his voice, as this was not like him, but I supposed maybe he was irritable because his knees were bothering him and causing him enough pain to lose sleep. We were all quiet for a moment, then he pushed back his seat from the table and went upstairs to his room.

When he didn't come down after an hour, I decided to see if he was feeling okay. I knocked on his bedroom door, and William invited me in. Sitting on the edge of his bed, with his hands folded on his lap, he looked like that same lost little boy who stood by the grave site not sure what to do next. I sat down beside him.

"So, what now?" he asked.

"What do you mean?"

"So, do I leave now?"

I was stunned. "Of course not. Why would you ask that?"

"Well, I know you said I could stay forever." He paused. "But I broke the rules."

I thought back to his comment at dinner, and I guess to him, his leaving the table registered as unkindness toward me. Watching his hopelessness, my heart ached for him, and I needed to help him understand. "Pop, rules might give us some order, but love and grace make life worth living. You belong here now. You are allowed to mess up just like any one of us. You are family, and we're not going anywhere without you. We threw away the sales receipt when we brought you home. We're keeping you."

THE PROMISE OLDER THAN MOSES

Keeping is what we long for and what God promises us. We hope, we wish, we pray for promises that we can count on, come rain or shine, to shelter our hearts and our being, our dreams and our doings. We want these promises to be kept whether we mess up (or think we did) or someone else does.

It's an age-old longing, older than Moses, this yearning for promises made and promises kept. In fact, it is Moses I think of when I think about promises: Moses, who was called to lead God's people out of slavery and to the promised land. Moses, who was called a friend of God. Moses, who would talk with God as a man talks with a friend (Exodus 33:11). But there's also Moses the doubter (Exodus 3:10–4:13) and murderer (Exodus 2:11–14), the very human Moses who got angry and afraid, felt disappointment and discouragement. I think of the Moses who experienced—just as William found in our home, and I discovered one stormy night in the Cairngorm Mountains—that God makes and keeps His promises to us, regardless of our faithfulness to Him.

The moment of Moses' story that stands out to me is when he pleaded with God to remember His promises (Exodus 33:12–17). Moses had been given God's Ten Commandments and had brought them down from Mount Sinai only to find that the people were not ready to receive them.

Tired of waiting in the wilderness on God and Moses, the people had made a golden calf from their bit jewelry—rings and earrings. They were worshipping their own creation, looking for promises they could control themselves or make and break as they saw fit instead of trusting in the promises of God, the promise to be led to a promised land.

Moses came upon the scene and, enraged at seeing the golden calf, threw down the Commandments written on tablets of stone. *How could the people not wait on God? How could they not see that even*

6

now God was bringing about all He'd offered? Pebbles and dust, shards and splinters of stone were strewn like broken promises at Moses' feet. Having just come from the glorious presence of God, he was heartbroken and devastated.

God was devastated, too, so shattered that He told Moses that maybe He should leave His people.

Oh no, no, Moses begs. *If You don't go with me, with us, how can I lead? Where will we go? Let me know Your ways. Let me see Your glory so I can know You.* "Then Moses said to him, 'If your Presence does not go with us, do not send us up from here. How will anyone know that you are pleased with me and with your people unless you go with us? What else will distinguish me and your people from all the other people on the face of the earth?'" (Exodus 33:15–16).

God, moved by Moses and unable to leave those He loved or resist their cries, had already planned a way to stay and to keep them. In the dust and the rubble of the broken tablets, His Word remained true, His promises would be kept. God looked on Moses as he begged not only to stay in God's presence but to see all of God's glory. God, whose heart was broken like those tablets of stone, began picking up all the pieces.

Imagine God, after having witnessed the rejection of the people He just rescued, saying to Moses, "I will have mercy . . . I will have compassion" (Exodus 33:19). It is as if God, having watched the people desecrate and decimate the shelter of His covering, was willing to offer those pieces of Himself again, collecting them, repositioning them. Then, in an act of great mercy, He told Moses to get new stones for new tablets on which the Word would be written for the people. Even when they had proven to be totally faithless, He remained willing to start all over again.

The shelter God made for Moses was the cleft of Horeb, a cleft meant not only for protection from the storms but for the chance to see His glory. What we learn from Moses, though, extends beyond

7

the scene with the Ten Commandments. There was a greater theme of God's promise and provision happening in that moment. Bible commentator Matthew Henry explains it this way:

> A full discovery of the glory of God would overwhelm even Moses himself. Man is mean and unworthy of it; weak and could not bear it; guilty and could not but dread it. The merciful display which is made in Christ Jesus alone can be borne by us. The Lord granted that which would abundantly satisfy. God's goodness is his glory; and he will have us to know him by the glory of his majesty. Upon the rock there was a fit place for Moses to view the goodness and glory of God. The rock in Horeb was typical of Christ the Rock; the refuge, salvation, and strength. Happy are they who stand upon this Rock. The cleft is an emblem of Christ as smitten, crucified, wounded, and slain.[1]

The cleft in Horeb for Moses is a symbol and pointer to Christ, who is the ultimate cleft, the Rock of Ages, cleft for us. As Henry explains, for Moses, the cleft was not just for his protection. It was also the sanctified place whereby God could let him see a glimpse of His glory, His majesty. And so it is with Christ, the One in whom God poured His glory and majesty so we could catch a glimpse of the Almighty and be kept safe by the abundance of His provision.

CHRIST IS THE CLEFT, THE KEEP

This is the shelter of all God's promises. God not only keeps His promises but He longs to keep us in them. As it was in those castles long ago, made of rock and stone, the very center tower was called the "keep" and provided shelter, a place of habitation, an operating station from which defense, under siege, was centered. Usually a well was built at the center of the keep so those sustained there could not only endure but thrive.

> *This is the shelter of all God's promises: God not only keeps His promises, but He longs to keep us in them.*

soft center

In God's kingdom, there is a keep, too, and it is Christ. How beautiful that God designed a way to provide such strength for us through the Person we crushed through our sin. How fitting that the rebellion of the Israelites, which brought about the destruction of God's tablets, is a reflection of the wounding we would cause to His Son. But light-years beyond these failures, our loving and promise-keeping Father would find a way to keep us, to say yes to us when we asked for forgiveness, protection, and a glimpse of His glory. That eternal Yes, that Shelter of the promise, is Christ.

In the face of some disappointments and discouragements, the apostle Paul reminded the Corinthians of this:

> For no matter how many promises God has made, they are "Yes" in Christ. And so through him the "Amen" is spoken by us to the glory of God. Now it is God who makes both us and you stand firm in Christ. He anointed us, set his seal of ownership on us, and put his Spirit in our hearts as a deposit, guaranteeing what is to come. (2 Corinthians 1:20–22)

Just rest for a moment in the beauty that comes with the phrase "He set his seal of ownership on us." God claimed us through

9

Christ—He has made an eternity-long commitment to us that He cannot break. But He didn't just put a seal on us and set us aside like a near-empty jar stuffed way back in the cupboard. No, God has made *many* promises to His people, and they all come back to Christ. Here's how another Bible commentator explains it:

> These promises are all "in" Christ; with and in whom could they be but in him, since he only existed when they were made, which was from everlasting? with and in whom should they be of right, but in him with whom the covenant, which contains these promises, were made, and who undertook the accomplishment of them? where could they be safe and secure but in him, in whose hands are the persons, grace, and glory of his people? not in Adam, nor in angels, nor in themselves, only in him . . . by whose blood, the covenant, and all the promises of it, are ratified and confirmed, and in whom, who is the truth of them, they are all fulfilled.[2]

But why would God do this? Why, when we break so many promises to Him? We build our own golden calves and break our word to God, our vows, our promises. We say we trust Him and believe in His promises when we need them or want something. But when things don't work out the way we think they should, or something bad happens, a storm comes, or we're left waiting for answers like an Israelite in the wilderness, we can be so unfaithful. Sometimes in our pain or in our panic we forget God, we forget His promises.

Why would God want to keep us and His promises to us when we mess up so badly?

The Bible reminds us of a truth we too often forget, a truth that shines as clear as daylight: *because God cannot help Himself.* The force of His righteousness and mercy, which were from everlasting and formed the covenant with us, are the unchanging foundation upon which His promises are built. God does not change, nor do the glories of His person and the salvation He engineered for us. God's promises are as dependable as He is. Because they *are* Him.

God's promises are as dependable as He is. Because they are Him.

He can not lie.

GOD'S PROMISES ARE NOT LIKE OURS

There is a story in the Old Testament of a prophet named Balaam whose donkey talks back to him (Numbers 22:22–35). Balaam may be a prophet, but he is a heathen one and not looking after the interests of God, not counting on God's promises or commending them. He's only after his own purposes and gain. Even Balaam's donkey sees he's in trouble, so when Balaam sets off on a road for his own agenda, the donkey stops, turns into a field, presses Balaam's foot against a wall in a narrow place, and even lies down, refusing to go forward.

Balaam, enraged, beats his donkey, who talks back: *Haven't you ridden me all your life and have I ever done this before? Why can't you take another look and see what's going on here?*

Such wise words: take another look and see what's really going on here.

What Balaam will learn, and eventually tell the people, is what's really going on: "God is not man, that he should lie, nor a son of man, that he should change his mind" (Numbers 23:19). This is not so much a statement of faith from Balaam, as even to the end he puts stock more in the promises of men and their riches than the promises of God. But

Balaam cannot help but recognize what is true: God cannot lie. And this from a man who, we're told, has no love for God or any desire to change his own self-serving ways. I love the fact that we are given those words not from a devout follower of our Father but rather from an outsider who recognizes the truth of who God is and that He does what He says He will do without exception.

As I studied the word *promise* in the Old Testament, I came across a very interesting fact. The two Hebrew words we translate into English as "promise" are the words *dabar*, meaning "to say," and *omer*, meaning "to speak." In other words, when God says something, when God speaks, that is as good as it gets. He means what He says, and He says what He means. It would appear as if we, humankind, had to invent the word *promise* because what we say or speak cannot always be trusted, so we upped the ante with a new word. But when God speaks, He cannot lie.

That's the foundation stone of this book. When God makes us a promise, He can never break it. If a heathen prophet can live by this understanding, how much more so can we whom God has restored?

That's the foundation stone of this book. When God makes us a promise, He can never break it.

THE STRUGGLE TO COUNT ON HIM

When I was visiting Scotland in the summer of 2009 to celebrate my mother's eightieth birthday, I saw again that there is an innate hope in our hearts that we can count on the promises we are given, whether we are five years old or eighty. My mom is a very care-ful—or *canny*, as we call it in Scotland—housewife. She has lived on a modest, fixed income for many years and knows how to balance a budget, but she had been taken in by several mail marketing schemes simply because they promised generous returns on purchases made through their catalogs. So her kitchen was piled high with foot cream from Holland and macaroons from Belgium. I tried to reason with my mom that I had seen television news reports exposing these scams. Yet this kind of suspicion was outside my mom's personal integrity to grasp. How could anyone make such bold claims without any inten-tion of remaining true to their word?

"How could they print something like that in black and white if it's not true?" she asked.

This is the primal struggle we have to deal with here on earth before we are able to move on to receive God's promises. We have to separate promises that may never be kept from God's promises, which will never be broken. We have a lifetime of experiencing deception, corruption, and embellishment on one side of the scales and a simple, profound promise on the other: God cannot lie. Our human experi-ence does not sync up with a heavenly truth.

We have to separate promises that may never be kept
from God's promises, which will never be broken.

I wonder if we have such a hard time believing this, resting in God's promises, because we have been lied to so many times, because so many earthly promises are broken. Think for a moment of the cultural climate in which we have grown up. We live in a day when

13

those who want to sell us something easily access us through television, radio, the Internet, and even our cell phones. We are told: If you follow this diet, you will lose twenty pounds in two days. If you use this face cream, you will look twenty years younger in two weeks. If you use this shampoo, your hair will be full and flowing as it sparkles and shimmers in the breeze.

The sensible part of us knows that such promises are nonsense, but isn't there another part of us that longs to believe miracles can actually happen? And don't we think at some level, *Surely these kinds of promises wouldn't be made if they weren't true?*

Culture has driven us to think of promises as personal fulfillment, when God's promises are not about us, but about Him and being saved by Him. God's promises are an expression of His holiness.

I remember watching television one night with my son, Christian, when he was almost five years old. It was getting close to Christmas, and we were facing the usual barrage of must-have toys. A commercial interrupted *The Grinch* to sell a new fishing rod for kids that guaranteed catching a fish within five minutes "or your money back."

Christian asked if he could have one.

I told him that his daddy and I would be glad to get him a fishing rod, but fishing is a learned skill, and no one can promise that you'll catch a fish in five minutes.

I'll never forget how Christian looked at me with his big brown eyes and said, "But they just said you can on television. They wouldn't lie, Mommy."

My heart ached for him as I realized that he was just beginning to taste what it's like to live in a culture that thrives on telling lies with no apologies. What a difference there is, however, between the promises made in sales pitches, among ourselves, and even the promises we make to ourselves, and the promises of God.

As I sat on the couch, while the people of Whoville and Little

Cindy Lou Who all ate "roast beast," I thought about my love for Christian. How much Barry and I want to keep him safe and healthy, see him happy and living with purpose and passion. How much we love to look in his eyes and see a part of ourselves there, but something more too, something unique and beautiful and surprising. How much we want to enjoy him forever—a new capacity in our hearts that God gave us through parenthood, a reflection of His love for us. Though we break God's heart at times, He loves us and says, *You can shatter Me like My Word on the stone tablets. You can leave Me in pieces, and I will still love you. I will hold on to you. I will create a place, a cleft in the rock for you, to keep you and on which you can steady yourself and stand.*

God keeps us not only to give us a future, but also to reflect His glory. He keeps His promises to us because He cannot help Himself. He cannot lie, and He is full of love for His creation.

God keeps us not only to give us a future, but also to reflect His glory. He keeps His promises to us because He cannot help Himself.

FROM THE CLEFT BACK TO THE GARDEN

From the very beginning, God made a promise and had a plan. You can trace His promises back to the garden of Eden. When Eve disobeyed God, when she ate the fruit from the tree of knowledge of good and evil and shared it with her husband, Adam, we lost our place in Paradise. Sin became our birthright. But God in His grace and mercy promised deliverance before He banished Adam and Eve, and us, from that perfect place of no pain, no worry, no storms. Genesis 3:14–15 captures the moment:

So the LORD God said to the serpent, "Because you have done this,

"Cursed are you above all the livestock
    and all the wild animals!
You will crawl on your belly
    and you will eat dust
    all the days of your life.
And I will put enmity
    between you and the woman,
    and between your offspring and hers;
he will crush your head,
    and you will strike his heel."

The promise was that the seed of Adam and Eve would crush Satan's head and destroy him for eternity. Satan would bruise Christ's heel, meaning there would be pain and suffering ahead for the Messiah. That seed is Christ Jesus. God's promise for you and me today is that there is a limit to the time that the enemy will be able to have free reign on this earth, and that even during that limited time and space, Christ Himself will walk with us.

Whenever I am faced with a difficult passage in my life or that of a friend, I remind myself again that we are travelers in this world, headed back to our true home with God. But we come upon detours in our journey. Each detour takes us from the garden to a cross on a hill, where Christ Himself paid the ultimate sacrifice so that we will be free. Even as Christ was placed in a grave carved into a cleft of rock, He went there as a fulfillment of God's promise to you and to me that death would be swallowed up in victory, for no grave could hold Him.

I can never forget that night I was in the Cairngorms, how I made my way in the dark into the cleft of the rock and found a place of shelter. We are each invited from the worst storms of our lives to find our safe hiding place in God. God provided shelter for Moses not in a moment of shining triumph but when his heart was broken by the faithlessness of those around him. When the people failed, God's glory caused Moses' face to shine as He reiterated His promises one more time. Our faithlessness does nothing to diminish God's faithfulness. Whatever God says, we can stake our lives on, and Christ came to show us who our Father is. In Christ all the promises of God are fulfilled, for no matter how many promises God has made, they are "yes" in Him (2 Corinthians 1:20).

Whatever God says, we can stake our lives on.

Isn't that beautiful? Isn't it so mysteriously complicated and yet so simple? Isn't that just like God to always come down to the most elemental way of things? In His creation, there is darkness and there is light. There is the beginning and an end, the heavens and earth, water and rock, body and blood, your broken heart and His.

Normally we doubt whether a promise maker will be a promise keeper when everything is completed. But the witness of the substitutionary atonement of Jesus is that God's most difficult promise has been kept. The Father is truly the only Promise Maker who is in earnest a Promise Keeper. A promise from God is a promise kept.

There are His promises and His unbreakable commitment to keep them.

There is Christ. There is yes.

Darlene EKG - $10

Marie

Farmers

Greg's mothers house sales
she moves on the 7th

2

PROVISION

I Don't Have Enough

THE PROMISE

*And my God will meet all your needs according to his glorious
riches in Christ Jesus.*

—PHILIPPIANS 4:19

Christian was about to turn four, and his father and I were in full
birthday-party-planning mode. As I mentioned, William, my
father-in-law, had been living with us since his wife died the previous year, so he was highly invested in this birthday bash as well. We
wanted to celebrate Christian and for him to know how very loved he
was. How do you show a lifetime of love in a moment, in a day? We
wondered this as we sat at the breakfast table, each with our own copy
of the local parenting magazine open to the classified section.

"What about a clown?" William suggested.

19

"That might be good," I said, "although sometimes clowns can be a little scary for younger kids."

"I think he'd like a jumpy-inflatable-castle thing," Barry said.

"Yes, those are fun," I agreed. "I've heard great things, too, about this guy who comes from the zoo with a selection of small animals and teaches the kids about them."

"How small?" Barry asked.

"Well . . . like raccoons and lizards and small snakes," I said.

"Snakes!" William shivered. "Man, I hate snakes."

"What about this?" Barry held up a magazine page open to a picture of two llamas.

"What do they do?" William asked.

"They give pony rides, except they are llamas, so llama rides, I guess," Barry replied.

"I like that," I said.

Finally we narrowed it down to six possibilities. Barry said he would make inquiries and see what was available for the date we wanted, and he'd check on the cost. I sent out the invitations and ordered the cake and prayed for a sunny day. As the birthday got closer, I asked Barry which entertainment option he had chosen.

Ah, he said, it would be a surprise.

The phrase "oh foolish Galatians" came to mind as I wondered why I wasn't asking more questions and what Barry would choose from all the outlandish options, but I ignored it.

So Christian's fourth birthday arrived, and the morning sun seemed to say everything would be picture-perfect. The party was scheduled from 2:00 p.m. to 5:00 p.m., and at 1:30 p.m. a van pulled into our driveway. The signage on its side said PARTY INFLATABLES.

"Great choice, Barry," I said. "Christian will love this!"

Barry looked a little confused. I thought of the impending stampede of four-year-olds about to flatten our lawn. Christian ran around the yard, beside himself with excitement as he saw the giant inflatable castle take shape. William stationed himself at the front door to welcome our guests as they began to arrive, and I showed the children and their moms into the backyard.

"Sheila!"

I heard William call my name with an edge of concern, and I hurried to the front door. He pointed down the driveway where two girls stood holding the reins of three ponies. Another girl stood on the doorstep.

"Hi!" I said. "Are these for the Walsh party?"

She assured me that they were, and I led them around the side of the house to the backyard. Christian and his friends were excited and lined up to take turns at riding the animals.

Okay, so Barry booked the castle and the ponies, I thought. *That's fun, because you don't turn four every day.*

"Sheila!"

I arrived back at the front door in time to see Crackles the clown wearing a fire-engine-red wig. A big red nose and loud horn announced her arrival with three short but profound blasts.

"Are you here for the Walsh party?" I asked in disbelief.

She replied with one deafening honk.

I decided this might be an opportune moment to ask Barry why half of Nashville's children party planners had stationed themselves at our house, but I didn't get that far.

"Sheila!"

I was almost afraid to answer the call. William stood at the door looking as if a truck had hit him as Jungle Jim began to unload his menagerie of small zoo animals. Before I had a chance to ask him the obligatory question, Penelope the face painter arrived.

Now we officially had a three-ring circus.

I'd love to tell you that the craziness ended there, but there was one more surprise. The children had all taken turns on the ponies and were painted every color under the sun. They had bounced up a storm, laughed at the clown's exceedingly bad jokes, and were now sitting on the floor in the den in a half circle to listen to Jungle Jim.

By this time, William was lying down, quietly muttering to himself. I heard the doorbell and thought seriously, *I may never answer the door again.* I turned the knob nervously and spied out from the small slit. I was greeted by a harried-looking man who apologized for being late. Behind him stood two huge llamas!

As the children filed out that day, they, one by one, declared it the best party they had ever attended.

The mothers did not look so thrilled. "What are we supposed to do now for our parties?" one asked. "Book the space shuttle?"

I muttered something about leaving it all up to Barry, the book of Galatians, and that I was sure we would never again have a party. Deep inside I knew their fears of wanting their parties not to disappoint their children or not to seem "enough." If only they had known that we were now officially broke!

When every last critter had been gathered up, including the six-foot-long albino python (which, by the way, had been wrapped around my neck like a killer scarf) and every horn had been silenced, I found Barry sitting in the den with his head in his hands.

"What on earth was that?" I asked. "We just had sixteen critters in our home, and I'm not even counting the clown!"

"I didn't mean to," he said.

"What do you mean?" I asked. "Did they all just volunteer their services?"

"Well," Barry said, looking stunned, "I asked them all to hold the date until I decided which one I wanted, and I forgot to get back to the others when I made my decision."

"So which one had you decided on?" I asked.

"The llamas," he replied. "Just the llamas."

We looked at each other and fell on the floor laughing.

"Well, none of the moms are speaking to me," I said, "but Christian sure had a great party!"

THE PROMISE TO PROVIDE

On Christian's fourth birthday, my little family had way too much to offer, but there have been times when we feared we wouldn't have enough—enough money, time, or energy.

Haven't you been there, that place of worry, fret, and fear when the provisions needed aren't at hand and aren't coming? Or maybe you've been in that place where there is a circus going on around you, with all kinds of things coming your way, just not what you really needed. You get lost in a pile of bills, feeling overwhelmed with everything that has to be taken care of and not enough resources to meet the needs. The demands of life can be overwhelming when you look at what you have and compare it to what you need. You can be left to wonder, *Is God listening? Does He see? Will He fix things?*

Where's the hope of that promise in Philippians 4:19, "And my God will meet all your needs"? And how do you live in the assurance of that promise?

It sounds so easy, after all, when someone says, "Just believe in God's promises."

Paul is writing this promise from house arrest in Rome to one of his favorite churches. The church in Philippi has sent a dear brother, Epaphroditus, to encourage Paul in his prison. Now Paul thanks them for their kindness and their monetary support in this time of need. His spirits have been lifted, and he responds with a sincere prayer for their blessing. This is a prayer from a love-filled heart that they be given what he holds dearest, the richest blessings found only in Christ.

Paul says in Philippians 4:18 that he is "amply supplied," meaning "filled up" or "supplied to the point of overflowing." This is what he is praying for them when he says "My God will meet all your needs." There will be no lack in what is really needed. Note that Paul makes no mention of their desires. At the end of this statement he says "according to his glorious riches in Christ Jesus" (v. 19). Some take this to mean reward in heaven, but it more likely means spiritual needs satisfied by the power that has been given to Jesus. "Riches" speaks of the abundance of Christ's provision. "Glory" speaks of the fullness of His power. He is saying God is faithful and will not disappoint. His provision will be in keeping with the wealth of His mercy demonstrated in Jesus Christ. He takes care of His own.

The fear we have is of running out or not having what is necessary when times get rough. The fear comes out of a belief that times will get to be unbearable and we will have unmet needs.

The promise is that God knows our needs and has been proven to provide abundantly beyond what we can rightly expect. Our sign in earnest is the abundant grace of Christ's gift—His life for us. How can we not trust in such a provision?

This provision means God will provide for our needs much more than we can ever imagine.

I don't know what situation you find yourself in today or what your specific needs are, whether financial, relational, spiritual, or if you long for healing. Perhaps you have needs in each of these areas. The desire to take care of ourselves is so deep within us. And when we can't, or when some great need outstrips our ability to handle it, the fear and desperation that set in can be brutal. The force of such need and fear can turn on you, like a hungry beast threatening to eat you alive.

It's a feeling Jesus was familiar with.

Jesus Knows Your Needs

It's the beginning of the third year of Jesus' ministry, and the disciples have been with Jesus through some tough situations. They've heard His teaching with authority, seen His love for the unlikeliest of people, and witnessed so many miracles—how He provided fine wine at the end of a wedding and health for Peter's mother-in-law. They've watched His every move and now are being sent out on their own:

> Calling the Twelve to him, he sent them out two by two and gave them authority over evil spirits.
>
> These were his instructions: "Take nothing for the journey except a staff—no bread, no bag, no money in your belts. Wear sandals but not an extra tunic. Whenever you enter a house, stay there until you leave that town. And if any place will not welcome you or listen to you, shake the dust off your feet when you leave, as a testimony against them."
>
> They went out and preached that people should repent. They drove out many demons and anointed many sick people with oil and healed them. (Mark 6:7–13)

The disciples marvel at Jesus' instructions. Maybe not so much the first instruction—to go out in twos. They know Jewish law (Deuteronomy 17:6) required at least two witnesses to verify a story; they probably feel comfort in each having a partner for the road, not being alone. But the other instructions? Those cause more concern: take very little, no money or food, just a staff presumably to ward off wild animals. (They should have been at Christian's party!) Accept the first place offered to them to stay, and remain there until finished in that town, no trying to upgrade the accommodations. *What was Jesus expecting? For them to beg their way through the villages?*

25

Most disconcerting is that the disciples are being sent by Christ to cast out demons and heal the sick. The Hebrew word used here for "sent" is *apostellein*, which indicates official representation. The disciples are being sent in Jesus' name, with His authority and power, holy ambassadors to represent His message and perform miracles. Now that's a responsibility. If a town receives them, Jesus said, it receives Him. If not, that town stands under the judgment of God for having rejected Christ. Where you encounter rejection, He added, shake off the dust from your sandals as you leave—a common practice for Jews leaving a Gentile area, but a first for leaving the homes of fellow Jews. Shaking off the dust upon exit would be shocking to any Jew who observed it, as it would in effect say to them that they were behaving as pagans.

So the instructions alone were a little daunting, but the mission? Overwhelming! For the disciples, it is one thing to watch Jesus conduct remarkable miracles, but it is quite another to be commissioned to do the same.

It is one thing to watch Jesus conduct remarkable miracles, but it is quite another to be commissioned to do the same.

How would you have felt? Imagine seeing Jesus turn water into wine at a wedding, heal the lame and the blind, and restore a man who had leprosy and another who had a withered hand. Then He sends you out in His name to do the same things. I can only imagine what was racing through the disciples' hearts and minds. I would have been saying to my partner, "You first. No, really, go ahead. You're a natural. You take the big diseases, and I'll take the coughs!"

The experience must have been amazing as the disciples saw God using their lives to do the things they had watched Jesus do: heal the sick, cast out demons, call many people to repentance. What a change from their previous jobs: pulling fish out of the sea, collecting taxes, guarding sheep. What an exciting moment when they all rejoined Jesus: "The apostles gathered around Jesus and reported to him all they had done and taught. Then, because so many people were coming and going that they did not even have a chance to eat, he said to them, 'Come with me by yourselves to a quiet place and get some rest'" (Mark 6:30–31).

I wonder how their conversations went in private, the group stealing away, eager to recount all that had happened. I can almost hear them interrupting one another with excitement to tell what they'd experienced. *Tell them, Peter, about the message you gave in that one town! You know, when the whole family repented and the father was sick and he was healed. It was just amazing! Oh, but wait till you hear what happened in the least likely place of all!*

Jesus must have been deeply moved by and excited for His friends, but we know He was wrestling with grief too. His heart was broken over the news just received that John the Baptist had been beheaded, because, we're told, not only had His friends brought good news of miracles and repentance, but John's disciples had told Christ about this grisly murder: "John's disciples came and took his body and buried it. Then they went and told Jesus" (Matthew 14:12).

Herod Antipas, ruler of the Jews, had heard about the things the disciples were doing in Jesus' name and was horrified. He had privately respected John and even listened to him preach. His wife, Herodias, on the other hand, hated John the Baptist. No wonder. John had publicly criticized her marriage to Herod, who had divorced his first wife to marry her—the wife of his half brother. To please Herodias, Herod arrested John but "protected him, knowing him to be a righteous and holy man" (Mark 6:20). Herodias tricked her husband, however, at his birthday party. She had her daughter dance in such a way that all the men in the banquet went wild. In an act of intoxicated good humor, Herod offered the girl half his kingdom. When she rejected the kingdom and instead asked for the head of John the Baptist on a platter, Herod knew he'd been ambushed. He had given his word at the party, so as a crowd looked on, he sent an executioner to John's cell with instruction to kill the Baptist and bring his head on a plate to the drunken crowd.

In the hours following the macabre scene, Herod became even more distraught. The disciples came and begged for John's body to bury it, and with them came word of the remarkable things they had been doing in Jesus' name. Herod was convinced that a man he had executed against his better judgment had now come back to haunt him: "Now Herod the tetrarch heard about all that was going on. And he was perplexed, because some were saying that John had been raised from the dead" (Luke 9:7).

The disciples must have been distraught too. John had given his life to prepare the way for Jesus—and his life ended in a barbaric way for a drunken crowd. Where was God? What about His promise to provide protection and care?

PROVISION IS NOT PERFECTION

Jesus teaches us an important lesson about God's promise to provide for us, but not in a sermon with words. Instead, He shows us this lesson with His very life and love and grief. Jesus is grieved, so grieved that He wants to get away.

Upon hearing the news of John's death, Jesus' heart is heavy. We see Him sink in spirit. He sees His disciples, exhausted from their first mission, and Jesus knows it's a moment to retreat. God's promises seem faded and distant. Things look bleak. They all need perspective. Mark 6:32 tells us, simply: "So they went away by themselves in a boat to a solitary place."

Do you see how Jesus meets us in our need? How He met the disciples? There are times when words don't help, when friends can't touch our grief. Our deepest need is to pull away with Christ—"Far from the Madding Crowd," as Thomas Hardy titled his book.

He understands fear and fatigue, disappointment and discouragement. Whatever you are facing, Jesus understands. He knows that heartbreak from worry and distress over provision, protection, and care in the everyday can eat at a person. He understands the pain when it seems that God is not keeping His end of the bargain. He understands that pain can be drastic, as in losing a friend, or more daily as in when the cupboards are empty and it's still a couple of weeks till payday. Or when an unexpected doctor's visit leaves you with a bill bigger than six months' income. Or when guests show up on your doorstep, needing a place to stay the night, and you only have so many beds. Or it can even be as frustrating as when your child tells you over breakfast that he's supposed to bring two dozen home-baked cookies to school that morning.

Each of us can get to the point where we are worn out stewing over how God will provide for us. But when we come to the end of ourselves, Jesus, our Cleft in the Rock, calls. *Come away with Me*, He says. *Find a quiet place with Me. Rest here with Me.*

When we come to the end of ourselves, Jesus, our Cleft in the Rock, calls. **Come away with Me.**

Can you imagine a kinder call from the chaos and demands of life than a call to escape it all with Jesus, with God? I wonder if this is one reason each Gospel account, even John's, which doesn't include the story of John the Baptist's beheading, makes a point about Jesus' retreat. Just as He in distress sought time with His Father, we can seek shelter from demands on our bodies, minds, and spirits with Him.

Even the witnesses around Jesus and the disciples, at a time of their great need, see this. And they follow.

SEE WHAT HE WILL DO

As Jesus and the disciples set sail for a remote place near the town of Bethsaida, the crowds run along the shoreline. They watch for Jesus and when they see the direction His boat is headed, they run faster, ahead of Him. Though Jesus is headed for a desolate place, the chasing crowd packs the shoreline by the time His boat arrives.

Mark 6:34 tells us that as Jesus sees the people on the shore, He has compassion on them. He doesn't see a tired, wanting, clamoring crowd, but sheep without a shepherd. Hungry sheep. Sheep who in a few hours will be grumbling for dinner. So for now the Lamb of God sits with the people. He is broken and yet full of love, spent and yet ready to spill out His broken heart, His very self as the spiritual bread the people crave. He begins to teach, and He feeds the people's hungry souls.

The disciples are astonished. They know Jesus is weary and sad over the news of John's death. The sting of John the Baptist's murder is still fresh for them too. As the sun begins to set, they urge Jesus to wrap up His teaching and send the people away. The disciples are hungry and they are tired too.

Every gospel writer tells us about Jesus' miracle of feeding a crowd of five thousand people on a hill from two fishes and five barley loaves. This miracle, after all, is the only one apart from the resurrection that is included in each of the four gospels. That fact alone pulls me in closer and makes me wonder what here is so important that every gospel writer includes it while leaving out other miracles from account to account? And why does each writer emphasize different, particular details?

Matthew, for instance, gives a short, condensed version of the events (14:13–21). Luke uniquely notes that the event happened in the region of Bethsaida (9:10–17); the other gospel writers do not identify the place. Mark makes a point that when Jesus feels compassion for the crowd on the hillside, it is as a shepherd for his sheep (6:33–44). John works in a sermon Jesus gave after the hillside events, to explain how He is the bread of life (6:1–14).

Taken together, these accounts seem to say, *This is more than a recording of a miracle. This is an undeniable message about who Christ is and what He can do.* There are also clues about what Jesus expects of us and a challenge to us about concentrating on what we have or don't have and about bringing both our blessing and our need to Him. All these things reside in how very human Jesus became and how much He understands about our needs.

You can imagine how the disciples must have felt, if you have ever been in that place where if your children, whom you love dearly, ask for one more thing. You will lose it, right? Or if you've ever wanted to throw the alarm across the room till it crashes into silence because you can't face the thought of everything the day ahead holds. Or if you've ever sat in a doctor's office and thought, *If I hear one more piece of bad news, I am done.* Or if you've ever been asked to do something that you know without a shadow of a doubt you simply don't have what it takes to do it.

This is where Philip might have been, for when Jesus asks him, "Where shall we buy bread for these people to eat?" (John 6:5), Philip gives an exasperated answer. *There's not enough!* he tells Jesus. *No way is there enough. Not even with a man's eight-month salary could we buy enough bread for each person here to have even a little to eat.* Can't you hear Philip thinking, *Do You get it, Lord? Do You really understand what's needed here?!*

Poor Philip. Poor us. So often when we are faced with need, we don't see, as John 6:6 says, that Jesus already knows what He is going to do. God already has a plan to keep His promise and provide.

THE PROMISE OF WHAT'S POSSIBLE

This is part of a test, Scripture tells us. Jesus sends us out to stand on God's promises and retreat with Him when we're discouraged—but then go back out again. Will we believe in what He promises to do through thick and thin, dinner or no dinner? Do we get it that when it comes to provision, we can do nothing on our own anyway? That only in Jesus' name, and by resting in Him, our Shelter, do we have something to stand upon, and that from that place anything is possible?

Jesus sends us out to stand on God's promises, and retreat with Him when we're discouraged—but then go back out again.

Not only Philip, but each of the disciples and a whole multitude are about to find out. The size of the crowd is remarkable, by the way. The Gospels tell us there are five thousand men, and you add in wives and children, widows and single women, and we are looking at a crowd of at least ten thousand people. How on earth could the disciples—who had no food with them, not even a pack of gum, so to speak—provide for all these people? The fact is, they can't, and that is the whole point. God is about to do what only God can do.

The disciples look at Jesus in disbelief as He asks, "How many loaves do you have?" They must have felt skeptical when He added, "Go and see" (Mark 6:38).

I've had those moments. So often I am overwhelmed by what I don't have instead of by what Christ has given me. I see that in my own life, but I see it powerfully illustrated many Sundays in my church through our associate minister, Neal Jeffrey.

Neal, a former All-American quarterback at Baylor University and NFL quarterback for the San Diego Chargers, has been a stutterer since childhood. When he wrote his first book, *If I Can, Y-Y-You Can!*, I received a copy of the manuscript to read. I was deeply moved by Neal's honesty and vulnerability. He knew that God had called him to preach, but that seemed impossible for a guy who stutters. He writes of the decision that changed everything:

> Finally one day I realized I could no longer say no to what God was calling me to do. So I decided, "I'm going to stand up and start talking even if everybody laughs at me. I've got something to say and I'm going to start saying it!"
>
> Do you know what happened when I made that decision? My whole life changed! Not because I stopped stuttering, because I didn't stop. My life changed when my attitude to my stuttering changed.
>
> It's about my answering God's call to give all I could give to become all I could be.[1]

What a huge lesson—a lesson not even the disciples can learn until they, too, answer their call. They have to undertake the somewhat embarrassing task of trying to find out in that huge crowd if anyone has food stashed away. It is John who fills in the details that the other three writers leave out, how another of the disciples, Andrew, Simon Peter's brother, speaks up: "Here is a boy with five small barley loaves and two small fish, but how far will they go among so many?" (John 6:9).

I'm sure I would have asked the same question as Andrew. All he had to show Jesus out of that vast crowd of people was a boy's packed lunch. What Andrew and the disciples learned, and what I am learning, too, is that how far the provisions will go is not the issue. The issue is, whose hands will they be in?

Jesus is getting ready to blow everyone away with God's answer. Jesus reaches for the cheap bread and tiny fish, the food of the poor. Mark 6:41 tells us, "Taking the five loaves and the two fish and looking up to heaven, he gave thanks and broke the loaves. Then he gave them to his disciples to set before the people. He also divided the two fish among them all."

The Greek word used here for blessing is *eulogeo*, from which we get our English word *eulogize*, meaning "to praise, and speak well of." When the Jews prayed before a meal, they saw it as an opportunity to praise God, not just for the meal before them, but also for who He is. So they did not pray, "For what we are about to receive may the Lord make us truly thankful." Their traditional prayer was, "Blessed are You, Lord our God, King of the world, who has caused bread to come forth out of the earth."

The prayer for provision granted says a lot about us, according to Dr. Ralph F. Wilson. In an online article called "Don't Ask the Blessing, Offer One," he notes:

> So how did we Christians end up blessing the food instead of God? Tradition? Habit? Some of the confusion may have come from a mistranslation of the passage I just quoted. In the King James Version, Matthew 26:26 reads: "And as they were eating, Jesus took bread,

and blessed *it*, and brake *it*, and gave *it* to the disciples, and said, 'Take, eat; this is my body.'" Notice how the tiny word "it" was added after the word "blessed"? The word "it" isn't part of the Greek text—that's why it's in italics in the King James Version. But "bless it" implies something far different than "bless God." That addition of one little word may have twisted the way we pray before meals into something Jesus didn't intend at all.[2]

I did not know that! But doesn't it make total sense? Why would we ask God to bless the food, when it is already blessed by His provision? It is God Himself we bless!

So Jesus blesses God, breaks the food, and gives it to the disciples to distribute to the crowd. And when all the people had eaten as much as they want, the disciples gather up everything that is left over in twelve baskets. The Greek word used here for "baskets" is *kophinos* and means "a large carrying basket." It's the same word used for the baskets that the Roman soldiers used to carry their equipment.

In other words, there are a lot of leftovers.

God Always Gives More

I wonder how many times the disciples had to come back to Jesus to get more as they distributed the food to such a huge crowd. Think about it. There were just twelve of them and perhaps ten thousand people. So they come back over and over and over again to refill their baskets, and each time I imagine the message going a little deeper:

Jesus can supply more than you will ever need.
Jesus can supply more than you will ever need.
Jesus can supply more than you will ever need.

35

With each of those reminders, I think on the details in this story: Jesus doesn't simply make enough for everyone, but so much more than enough. He doesn't choose a master chef or big food distributor of the day, but a poor boy and his little lunch. Where some people are not valued or even neglected and ignored, as the women and children on the hillside that day (as seen by the fact that only the men are counted), Jesus uses them for His miracles and provides for them anyway. God, after all, has Jesus not only looking out for our immediate needs, but our ultimate needs too: our knowledge that in Christ we have belonging and purpose, value and worth.

Christ then shows how we remind ourselves of that. After all the crowds have been fed, the immediate needs met, He once again retreats. He shows us that even the Son needs His Father for rest, restoration, for God's providence, glory, and shelter.

And so Jesus, exhausted, goes into the mountains to be alone with God.

The disciples, meanwhile, return to the boat and set sail for Capernaum. They are tired from all they have been through: wonders and trials on the road in ministry, heartbreak and fear over the murder of their friend John the Baptist, stress from the crowds chasing them, amazement at another miracle by Jesus, physical exhaustion from the food distribution and crowd control of five to ten thousand people. Of course, in this state during the night, a storm blows up and the waves became very rough—and isn't that just how life goes? You are taxed and pressed by demands, there are worries and concerns about how all is going to work out, and just when some relief comes, so does another storm.

So the wind is blowing and the waves crashing, and the disciples are trying to keep themselves together. They are rowing and rowing, straining and striving to stay afloat. Exhaustion adds to their fatigue.

And then they spot a figure approaching them—a man walking on the water.

They are terrified. Their hearts, like their little boat, are battered and sinking deep into confusion

Then Jesus identifies Himself: "It is I; don't be afraid" (John 6:20).

Eagerly, the disciples pull Him into the boat, and John 6:21 tells us that immediately they are at the land to which they were going. Not only has Jesus gotten them through the storm, but He's gone further and delivered them to their destination.

By morning, the crowds, astonished by the account rushing through the region of the divine feast He provided, look for Jesus because they know there is only one boat and Jesus didn't get in it. When they can't find Him, they get in their own boats and sail to Capernaum. When they find Jesus, they want to know how He got there. More, they want to know what they should do now that they've seen this astonishing act of God. Their astonishment is rooted in disbelief, and they ask for yet another sign. It's hard to believe that after all they've witnessed, they still want a sign. (Are we so different?) They say that they have the right to a sign, because didn't Moses provide manna for their ancestors in the wilderness?

Jesus says to them, "I tell you the truth, it is not Moses who has given you the bread from heaven, but it is my Father who gives you the true bread from heaven. For the bread of God is he who comes down from heaven and gives life to the world" (John 6:32–33). In the feeding of the five thousand, the miraculous bread—more bountiful than anyone could ever eat—is a symbol of Jesus Himself, the divine sustenance that comes from nothing and fulfills our every need . . . and then some! Christ's answer to the crowd that day is His answer to us: "I am the bread of life. He who comes to me will never go hungry, and he who believes in me will never be thirsty" (John 6:35).

Jesus tells them, as He tells us:

I am everything you need.
I am everything you need.
I am everything you need.

Jesus doesn't simply supply our daily bread. He *is* our daily bread.

> *Jesus doesn't simply supply our daily*
> *bread. He is our daily bread.*

A PROMISE FOR ALL TIME

There is no need we have that God is not able and willing to meet. God does not need our money or our time and resources, but He invites us into this divine adventure of partnering with Him to see what only He can do. In His grace, He loves to work through us. We can spend the rest of our lives looking at what we do not have, or we can bring everything we have and are to Him and watch miracles take place.

"My God will meet all your needs according to his glorious riches in Christ Jesus" (Philippians 4:19). We see in this promise verse that we work hand in hand with heaven: we see a need and meet it, and heaven sees all our needs and meets those. That's what Paul was saying when he wrote this promise to the church in Philippi. He was commending them for the way they had poured out their resources to help him and expressing his confidence that God who knows their needs would more than meet them. Paul was quick to clarify, though, that the point was not so much that he needed them to give but rather that God saw their loving sacrifice and participation in the ways of the kingdom of God. "Not that I am looking for a gift, but I am looking for what may be credited to your account" (Philippians 4:17).

This is a glorious promise! We give, like the boy on the mountainside, out of the little we have, and God in His grace and glory gives out of His limitless supply.

The miracle on the mountainside says, *Don't be consumed by what you don't have. Just bring what you do have to Jesus and watch Him do what only He can do.*

And my God will meet all your needs.

Jesus says to all of us, no matter what we are facing right now:

I am enough.
I am enough.
I am more than enough.

3

PEACE

I'm Afraid and Feel Alone

THE PROMISE

Peace I leave with you; my peace I give you.

—JOHN 14:27

I woke up that Saturday morning thinking that I should study but deciding almost immediately that I wouldn't. I could see that it was such a pretty day outside my college dorm room window, and after days and days of dreary rain and gray skies, I was excited to be out in the fresh air and sunshine. I was in my final year at London Bible College (now called London School of Theology), and the pressure was on to finish well. I had studied hard, so I decided that a day away from books and library shelves was just what I needed.

After a quick shower, I dressed and walked to the station to catch a train to central London. Having been raised in a small town on the west coast of Scotland, I was in love with everything that London

41

offered: I had student tickets to Sadler's Wells Ballet Company, the opera, museums, and art galleries, each presenting the finest that could be seen or heard.

I got off the train at Harrow-on-the-Hill and took the underground rail, or Tube as we call it, into South Kensington. It was the perfect day for a picnic, so I bought a sandwich and a soda and decided to make my way to St. James's Park. I put my college sweatshirt on the grass at the base of a huge oak tree, sat down, and leaned back against a well-worn trunk.

I love to people-watch, and a London park in May has plenty to see, from little old ladies walking little old dogs to musicians playing their version of a Simon and Garfunkel song. As I scanned the manicured grounds, my eyes met those of a man in his sixties. Our eye contact was brief as he immediately lowered his gaze to the grass. For some reason, something about this man touched me deeply. I tried not to stare at him, but I kept being drawn back. He wore an old coat, even though it was a warm day, and it was tied at the waist by a piece of rope. At his feet were two plastic shopping bags. It's a safe bet to say he was homeless. As I looked at his hands gently folded on his lap, I talked to God about him. I knew nothing about his story but was deeply aware that God knew every line.

After a few moments he looked up at me and smiled. I wandered over to where he was sitting and asked if I might join him, and he agreed. I asked if he'd had lunch, and when he said that he had not, I offered him half of my sandwich, which he took.

"I love it here," I said. "It's so full of life."

He just smiled.

"I sometimes come here just to feed the ducks," I continued. "They always seem to be starving."

He smiled. "I think you'll find they are better fed than many people you might encounter in this park."

42

His voice was gentle but compelling.

"So, are you a student?" he asked.

"Yes, I'm at Bible College," I answered. "I want to be a missionary in India."

"That is a very noble calling," he said with a smile.

"May I ask you about your life, sir?"

He looked at me with the saddest eyes I had ever encountered and told me his story. At one time he had been a physician on Harley Street, one of the most famous streets in London, with a reputation worldwide as a center of private medical excellence. Through a series of poor choices and an addiction to alcohol and prescription medicine, this gentle man in a coat frayed at the edges told me he had lost his marriage and family, his medical license and career. He went from being a man who earned a huge salary and the respect of his peers to someone people avoided.

Then he said something I have never forgotten. He said that he was walking along Oxford Street one day when he passed a store that had mirrored doors. Out of the corner of his eye, he glimpsed something that caused him to take a second look.

"I saw an old man in a dirty shirt and unkempt hair," he said, "and as my distaste for him rose, I realized that it was me. This is what I had become."

THE PROMISE OF PEACE

My new friend in the park had become someone unrecognizable even to himself, isolated and avoided. He lived in a place of unrest, loneliness, and self-loathing.

Do you know a place like this? Have you, too, found yourself tormented by life, in turmoil over the self-hatred you feel, longing for peace, the kind of perfect peace that only Christ promises and can deliver? What does it look like, this peace that Jesus promised when He said, "Peace I leave with you; my peace I give you" (John 14:27)? The Greek word used here for "peace" is *eirene*, which means "a state of untroubled, undisturbed well-being." Is such a thing possible in this world? Is it a peace that can shore us up when the storms of life leave us tattered, broken, or alone?

One man in the Bible, known as the Gadarene demoniac, must have wondered these things. Like my friend in St. James's Park, he also lived in a place of unrest. He, too, had become what he loathed and certainly society loathed, a man unkempt and unclean, living in isolation and fear—a place where most believe God does not abide. But it is a place where He promises to meet us, bringing peace to drive out the demons of vexation and worry, torment and unrest, loneliness and self-hatred.

Though the Gadarene demoniac and the man in St. James's Park had quite different life experiences, they shared common, agonizing ground. For starters, people avoided eye contact with them. With my friend in the park, people saw only a homeless person. In the Gadarene demoniac, a man struggling to survive amid the home of the dead, people saw only a social outcast of the worst kind.

What brought these men to their places of torment, isolation, and unrest, places where they felt our most primal fear of being alone in this world?

Beneath This Thing I've Become

Also known as the "man of the tombs" or, as some Bible translations call him, the "Gergesene demoniac," the Gadarene demoniac lived as an exile, as an attacker as well as one attacked. Take a look at his story in Mark 5:1–15:

> They went across the lake to the region of the Gerasenes. When Jesus got out of the boat, a man with an evil spirit came from the

tombs to meet him. This man lived in the tombs, and no one could bind him any more, not even with a chain. For he had often been chained hand and foot, but he tore the chains apart and broke the irons on his feet. No one was strong enough to subdue him. Night and day among the tombs and in the hills he would cry out and cut himself with stones.

When he saw Jesus from a distance, he ran and fell on his knees in front of him. He shouted at the top of his voice, "What do you want with me, Jesus, Son of the Most High God? Swear to God that you won't torture me!" For Jesus had said to him, "Come out of this man, you evil spirit!"

Then Jesus asked him, "What is your name?"

"My name is Legion," he replied, "for we are many." And he begged Jesus again and again not to send them out of the area.

A large herd of pigs was feeding on the nearby hillside. The demons begged Jesus, "Send us among the pigs; allow us to go into them." He gave them permission, and the evil spirits came out and went into the pigs. The herd, about two thousand in number, rushed down the steep bank into the lake and were drowned.

Those tending the pigs ran off and reported this in the town and countryside, and the people went out to see what had happened. When they came to Jesus, they saw the man who had been possessed by the legion of demons, sitting there, dressed and in his right mind; and they were afraid.

Scripture doesn't explain either the physical or mental process of demon possession or how this man ended up in such a wretched condition. When we meet him he is out of control and in torment. The tombs that had become his home were most likely caves cut into the side of the hill that would offer shelter when the wind, coming off the sea, would cut like a knife. A tempest raged within this poor man too. We read that his demon possession had led to inhuman strength so that no matter how many times he was bound or shackled by irons, he ripped them apart as if they were paper chains made by children.

Equally gruesome to what was happening inside of the Gadarene demoniac was the place in which he lived. The Jews considered the Gadarenes, the land on the eastern shore of Galilee, a detestable place. It was unfriendly territory on many levels, not the least of which was that it was an area of pagan, cult worship. The pagans' favorite animal to sacrifice was the pig, which was an unclean animal to the Jews, so with herds of pigs about, the place was an abomination to any Jew.

It is to this area, across the Galilee, that Jesus sails to meet the man of the tombs. Do you think that is any coincidence?

His disciples might have wondered. They were not at all happy about heading to the Gadarenes. And the crossing there was no plea-sure cruise either. They came upon stormy seas that night, a storm so fierce that their boat began to sink. The disciples thought they would surely die: "A furious squall came up, and the waves broke over the boat, so that it was nearly swamped" (Mark 4:37).

Yet as the waves crashed against the boat and filled it, as if trying to overpower and possess it, Jesus remained fast asleep in the stern. Imagine being one of the disciples, crossing a storm-tossed sea in a dinghy toward a land of demons and occult worship, inhabited by potentially thousands of unclean pigs and tombs to mark countless corpses. It was a Jewish nightmare.

It is in this state of mind and battling the storm-tossed waters that the disciples, panicked, wake Jesus. They ask Him, "Don't You even care about the fact that they we're all about to drown?"

Jesus stands up and speaks peace to the waves. "Quiet!" He says. "Be still!" (Mark 4:39). The waves still, and the sea suddenly becomes perfectly calm.

The disciples became afraid, mumbling to one another, "Who is this that even the wind and sea obey Him?"

They have no idea that they are about to witness the radical truth that when Christ speaks to storms outside and inside the human heart, both obey.

> *When Christ speaks to storms outside and inside the human heart, both obey.*

For We Are Many

I can picture what this scene must have felt like to the disciples, their version of Tolkien's Mordor and Dante's hell wrapped in the sinuous folds of black skies and the reek of evil and spiritual malice. My heart truly goes out to them. But what I find most moving in this account is that as soon as Jesus is on the horizon, the man of the tombs sees Him and runs to fall down before Him. This man's actions completely change the tone of the scene as the disciples' fears become incarnate in this demon-possessed man. How does the demoniac know who Jesus is? Could it be that for the first time ever he feels the demons within him recoil and cower, and in that moment he realizes the possibility of peace?

Have you ever been in a situation like that, in the worst setting possible and totally without hope? As far as you can tell, God has forgotten you. Maybe your life feels like a wasteland, or worse, you, too, feel tormented. Perhaps you have made some devastating choices that have led you to places you never thought you would go and alienated those who have loved you. Hopelessness is a devastating place to live, isolating and cold. Whether you find yourself in a place like that through choices of your own or the choices of others, the horizon is barren and bleak if you feel no hope at all. Without hope, the human spirit begins to check out of life.

Certainly this man of the tombs is dwelling in the land of the dead—not just of the physically dead who are his neighbors and bedfellows, but in the dead state of his emotions and spirituality too. And the demons are used to ruling there.

That's why, when the demons in the man feel the presence of Christ step off the boat, they recoil, and the possessed man rushes to the feet of the Lord: "When he saw Jesus from a distance, he ran and fell on his knees in front of him. He shouted at the top of his voice, 'What do you want from me, Jesus, Son of the Most High God? Swear to God that you won't torture me!'" (Mark 5:6–7).

Jesus is not into negotiations. The demons cry in response to Christ's command to them: "Come out of this man, you evil spirit!" (Mark 5:8).

It's clear from the passage that the demons do not immediately obey Jesus, so He asks them for their name. They reply, "My name is Legion, for we are many" (Mark 5:9).

A legion was the largest unit of the Roman army, consisting of six thousand men. Most commentators agree that this does not necessarily mean that the man was possessed by six thousand demons but that the number was obviously large. They beg Christ not to banish them to what they know their eternal destiny will be. They ask Jesus to let them stay in this land where they have wreaked so much havoc. They don't ask to be allowed to enter another man, knowing that Christ will never allow that, but rather to enter a herd of pigs.

It is quite a scene as this vast hoard of demons leave one poor, battered man and enter a herd of two thousand pigs that proceed to run squealing down a cliff and into the sea.

You Can Drown in Unrest

Geographers conclude that the most likely location for the leap of the swine into the sea would have been a strip of steep coastline near Gergesa, a smaller, less important town of that Gadarenes area on the east side of the Sea of Galilee. This would fit another suggestion that Matthew was a native of that region and that is why he pinpoints the exact place, while Mark and Luke simply refer to a general location for their Greek and Roman readers. Gergesa was small and relatively unknown, while Gadara was a Greek city of some importance.

This steep coastline is the kind of territory that if you started to run down you would not be able to stop.

We have a hill like that where I grew up in Scotland. Three sides of the hill are easily navigated up and down, but one is so steep that once you commit to it, you take whatever befalls you at the bottom.

One warm, sunny Saturday, my mom, sister, brother, and I were having a picnic there with friends. All the children wanted to climb the steeper side of the hill, and we were told in no uncertain terms that if we climbed to the top that way, we should not even consider coming back down on anything else but the three gentle sides. I'm not sure what it is in me that filters that kind of information as a challenge rather than a warning, but it appears to be firmly grafted in my DNA.

When we all finally scrambled to the top, the view was spectacular, and then it was time to head back down for our picnic. My sister, Frances, saw that I was not following her to one of the safe sides and reminded me of the dire warning. I assured her that I was no mere mortal—I knew I could do it.

Before anyone had a chance to physically restrain me, I took off. Within about three seconds I knew that I was in trouble. I couldn't slow down but instead was running faster and faster like a runaway train.

I heard someone shout, "Look out, Sheila!"

I raised my eyes off my smoking feet just long enough to see that I was headed straight for an enormous thornbush.

There was nothing I could do to avoid it.

It took three of the adults to pull me from the bush, and my mom declares that days later she still found thorns on me.

Certain hills, I learned, are not made for running unless you are willing to accept the consequences when you reach the bottom.

Well, that day at the Gadarenes was no different as two thousand pigs met their fate.

The sea, which had been so stormy and at unrest just hours before, gobbled up the squealing, racing, demon-possessed pigs. The chaos of the demons took them to the bottom of the sea. Hundreds after hundreds of pigs—two thousand in total, the Scripture says (Mark 5:13)—fell off the edge of the cliff and drowned.

Dressed and in His Right Mind

If I were one of the disciples, I would have been reaching for the Advil at this point. Just when you think life with Jesus can't get any more unpredictable, you are confronted with today's menu. The moment you step off a boat, a crazed, demon-possessed man rushes you, only to have his internal tormenters flinging pigs off a cliff within moments. And yet, for all this, as crazy as the scene is at the cliffs, in the presence of Jesus is total peace. I imagine Christ looking upon the man, ragged and fatigued to his very soul, prostrate in the dirt. For the first time in very long time, he is serene, quiet at the feet of Christ. The man who had torn his clothes and cut his flesh is now "dressed and in his right mind" (Mark 5:15).

The men who are in charge of the pigs have just lost their day job in one fell swoop, so they run into town to report what had happened. We read in Mark 5:14–17 that when a large crowd returns to the scene and sees this wild man now at peace, they are afraid. How ironic. This superstitious crowd is more afraid of this new situation than the monster who had cried out in the night. They are familiar with evil but have no reference point for the kingdom of God.

As for the man who has been set free, he begs to follow Jesus. He knows what darkness feels like, and he knows what Christ had done. But Jesus says no. He leaves this man as perhaps the first convert among the Gentiles to tell his story. This grateful servant sets out on his first missionary trip: "So the man went away and began to tell in the Decapolis how much Jesus had done for him. And all the people were amazed" (Mark 5:20). *Becomes a witness*

I wonder how the man felt as he watched Jesus walk away and return to the boat. As the figure of the One who had saved his life and restored his soul became smaller and smaller, one thing must have been crystal clear: at the name of Jesus, every knee shall bow. A vast host of hatred had torn him apart, and then Jesus Christ showed up and the evil spirits had to leave. We don't know how long a life the man of the tombs lived after his exorcism, but I am confident he became a radical disciple. If you have tasted of hell, you cling to the Lord of heaven.

Within twenty-four hours, the disciples witnessed that Christ has power over the storms that rage in the world and within the human spirit. They watched as Jesus spoke peace, turning a raging sea into placid waters, and they witnessed the most violent man they had encountered so far being set free. The constant was the presence of Christ. As you reflect on your own life, how long has the storm been raging around you? Perhaps like the disciples you have cried out, *Don't You see what's happening here? Don't You care that I'm about to drown?* Perhaps, more isolating and brutal, the storm that rages is inside your soul. That day, the disciples witnessed that the shelter Christ not only offers, but *is*, brings peace.

The disciples witnessed that the shelter Christ
not only offers, but is, brings peace.

FROM OUR OWN TOMBS

The torment of unrest that so many of us suffer has profoundly impacted my own life because I personally have known the man of the tombs.

He was my father.

I remember the first time that I heard Bob Bennett's song "Man of the Tombs" that tells of the demon-possessed man. I was attending a conference in Orange County, California, in January 1993. On the last day, the speaker played this song as a final tag to his message. Look at the words of the song:

> Man of the tombs,
> He lives in a place where no one goes
> And he tears at himself
> And lives with a pain that no one knows
> He counts himself dead among the living
> He knows no mercy and no forgiving
> Deep in the night he's driven to cry out loud
> Can you hear him cry out loud?
>
> Man of the tombs
> Possessed by an unseen enemy
> He breaks every chain
> And mistakes his freedom for being free

Shame and shamelessness equally there
Like a random toss of a coin in the air
Man of the tombs, he's driven to cry out loud

Underneath this thing that I've become
A fading memory of flesh and blood
I curse the womb, I bless the grave
I've lost my heart, I cannot be saved
Like those who fear me, I'm afraid
Like those I've hurt, I can feel pain
Naked now before my sin
And these stones that cut against my skin
Some try to touch me, but no one can
For man of the tombs I am[1]

I cannot remember what the conference speaker's message was about, but hearing the song that day, I sobbed at a depth that made no sense to me. It was embarrassing.

Now don't get me wrong: the song is great, and Bob is a fabulous writer. But I was being drawn into a place that felt like such a primal wound, it seemed out of proportion to the story the song told. I decided that I was just tired and thought no more about it, but the lyrics kept coming back to me. I bought Bob's *The View from Here* cassette (yes, those were the days of cassettes) and played it over and over. Each time I heard it, I would feel a deep sadness for this madman who knew no mercy, no forgiveness, and so much unrest and torment. Over the years I have touched base with Bob a few times, as I didn't want to lose contact with someone who has so profoundly impacted me.

As far as I am aware, I have never met a demon-possessed person. And yet, just as I was drawn to the homeless man in the park when I was a student in London, I have been drawn to this man who met

Jesus at the shoreline and finally found peace. One line in particular in Bob's lyrics continues to stop me dead in my tracks: "Some try to touch me but no one can / For man of the tombs I am."

I understand the isolation and despair that those words represent. As a child, I tried so hard to touch my dad, but I couldn't make him well again.

My dad was thirty-four years old when a brain aneurysm robbed him of the ability to speak and paralyzed his left side. This wonderful daddy, who loved me very much, became a man of the tombs through no choice of his own. The impact of the damage to his brain seemed to come in waves. One moment he would be "dressed and in his right mind" and the next, a confusing and angry stranger.

When he was himself, in his right mind, he would weep, understanding that at times he was a frightening stranger to his family and himself.

One of my most painful memories is the look in his eyes the last time I ever saw him alive. It was not the look of a loving father but the terrifying stare of a wild man who wanted to hurt me. Instead of allowing him to bring his cane down on my skull, I pulled it from him, and he fell to the floor, screaming like an animal.

He was taken away that day and died shortly after in a psychiatric hospital.

I understand now, as an adult, what I couldn't as a child, that my dad was ill and had no control over his rage. Over the years God has brought so much healing to my heart in this wound. My enduring sadness, though, has always been wondering what it was like to feel trapped inside a body that betrayed you daily. I was able to receive the peace that understanding brings, but what of my father? What peace had he been able to know? It was only when I returned in 2008 to the place where my father took his last steps on this earth that I believe God answered that question. My father did not die in a hospital bed but in a river behind the hospital. He had escaped that night, and the doctors were unable to determine whether he had slipped and fallen in or saw this as the way out of the caves of his illness.

I never wanted to walk that shoreline, but I found myself there one day. As I stood at the place of nightmares, I felt Christ say to me, *I was there that night. Your father went from this earth to My arms, and I carried him all the way home.*

> *Down at the shoreline*
> *Two sets of footprints meet*
> *One voice is screaming*
> *Another voice begins to speak*
> *In only a moment and only a word*
> *The evil departs like a thundering herd*
> *Man of the tombs, he hears this cry out loud.*
>
> *Underneath this thing that you've become*
> *I see a man of flesh and blood*
> *I give you life beyond the grave*
> *I heal your heart, I come to save*
> *No need to fear, be not afraid*
> *This Man of sorrows knows your pain*
> *I come to take away your sin*
> *And bear its marks upon My skin*
> *When no one can touch you, still I can*
> *For Son of God I am.*[2]

Perhaps this kind of torment has touched your life.

For me, I now understand my affinity to those who have another story to tell apart from the one that seems to be true about their lives. I have always been drawn to broken stories. For many years I felt that

I had failed my dad by not saving him and that saving another would possibly give me a measure of peace.

I know, as the man of the tombs learned and the disciples and every tormented soul, that only Christ can save, only He can bring peace. I can still be a friend who sees beyond what appears to be true, and a traveling companion on the journey home. Along the journey I'm sure to see many tormented lives in this world and to encounter my own unrest from time to time. Christ promises us that life here doesn't have to be this way, though. We have but to look for Him on the horizon and run to Him, ask for His peace. He can bring it with just a word, only a glance.

He sees us in the tombs and longs to take us to a better place, a place of peace.

Underneath this thing that I once was
Now I'm a man of flesh and blood
I have a life beyond the grave
I found my heart, I can now be saved
No need to fear, I am not afraid
This Man of sorrows took my pain
He comes to take away our sin
And bear its marks upon His skin
I'm telling you this story because
Man of the tombs I was.[3]

4

CONFIDENCE

I Can't See God's Plan in This Pain

THE PROMISE

And we know that in all things God works for the good of those who love him, who have been called according to his purpose.

—ROMANS 8:28

I will never forget a couple I interviewed many years ago on *The 700 Club* on the Christian Broadcasting Network. On the surface they looked like a typical Christian family. They had two small children, and the dad was involved in the leadership of their church. He also had another secret life where he acted out his homosexual desires. His wife had no idea about this part of her husband's life until she got very sick. At first they thought she had a bad case of the flu, and she was taken into the hospital to try to regulate her fever and fluids. While she was there, her husband learned from his doctor that he was HIV positive.

In utter despair, he realized that not only did he have the disease, but he had also most likely passed it on to his wife. His doctor made it clear that he had to tell her. So he bought a gun and drove to the hospital with the intention of telling his wife, facing her disgust, and then finding a quiet place to kill himself. But God had other plans.

As this husband sat by his wife's bed with tears pouring down his face, afraid to look into her eyes, he told her his story, the part of his life he had hidden from her for so long. He waited for her words to cut his soul to ribbons, but instead she reached out and took his hand. He looked up and saw that tears were pouring down her cheeks too. She said, "Do you realize that this is the first time in our marriage I feel there is no distance between us—just the truth?"

It was very humbling to listen to this couple share a story of such severe mercy and redemption. They were both HIV positive, and yet God—in the way only He can—had used the husband's terrible secret to bring them closer to His heart and to each other. At the worst moment of their lives, when no good could possibly be found, they were surprised by the grace of God and that they could take shelter under His promise—that He alone can bring good out of the greatest heartaches in life.

THE PROMISE OF PURPOSE

Have you ever had a moment when you were so overwhelmed by shame that it was impossible to imagine God bringing any good from it? Most of our shame-filled moments are not life-and-death, as they were for this couple, but they can cripple us into believing that we have no hope.

Within the church, shame has an extra, even more potent layer. If we have fallen into any kind of sin that becomes public within our community, we are judged and often excluded. I saw this happen with a dear friend. When she needed grace the most, her community sidelined and isolated her, adding an extra layer of cruelty to the bitter shame she felt.

So when it comes to despair and hopelessness and the way they can bear down upon us and suffocate us, what do we make of God's promise in Romans 8:28: "And we know that in all things God works for the good of those who love him, who have been called according to his purpose"?

Can God use even the worst circumstances in life for good, to bring us closer to Him? Do we really believe He will take the most unlikely events and painful moments of life to bring us closer to His heart? Does anything fall outside that powerful promise of comfort and affirmation—that we are valued by Him, that our lives mean something and are precious, and that God will redeem everything for our good, a greater good? That is the confident assertion of this promise: God will use *all* things for good.

And we know that in all things God works for the good of those who love him, who have been called according to his purpose.

The epistle to the Romans is focused entirely on condemnation and righteousness. The struggle the early church was facing is no different from what we face today. The problem is we keep looking to ourselves for this righteousness, and none of us is completely righteous. This is what the legalism is all about. Paul tells these early Christians and us that yes, we are all condemned by the law, and there are plenty of people available to remind us how unworthy we are. Then Paul says at the very beginning of chapter 8 that those who are in Christ have no condemnation. The spirit of law is sin and death, but we have the Spirit of life. He is telling the Romans, and us, to leave sin and death behind and embrace life. Ours is not a spirit of slavery but the Spirit of adoption into the family of God.

In Romans 8:27, Paul tells us that the Spirit knows our hearts and minds and He prays for us. On this foundation Paul boldly assures us that everything will work out. Rest assured God is at work in our lives. The first part of this sentence can be translated two ways. God is the one who is working all things together for good. Or all things are working for the good of those who are godly. Actually both readings are true and lead to the same conclusion. For those who are godly, all things work out for the good because God is actively working all things out for those who are His.

Paul puts this concept into perspective by clarifying who we are. We are the ones who have been selected by God specifically for His purposes. Therefore God makes all things, good or bad, work together to bring about His purposes, which are indeed good. The result should be confidence in the work of God. If we patiently wait, we will see the unfolding of these various experiences into the establishment of His purposes. Our confidence flows out of His steadfastness.

That road, however, can be a strange one. Perhaps no one knew that better than a woman who had spent most of her life looking for love and instead gave away pieces of her soul until one day she met a man who didn't want just a sliver or a slice.

He wanted it all.

Hope for the Most Unlikely One

Jesus had many fascinating encounters with women in the Gospel accounts, but His meeting with a Samaritan woman at the end of a hot and exhausting day is one of the most powerful.

The chance that they met at all would seem nothing less than amazing to this woman, revolutionary even. But with Jesus, we can know it wasn't a chance meeting. He sought her, even though she had two strikes against her. First, she was a Samaritan—and the Jews nurtured a pungent hatred for the Samaritans. Second, she was a woman—and women were not esteemed in the culture of the time.

To understand why the pure-blood Jews hated the Samaritans, you have to go back to 729 BC, when Assyrian settlers captured the ten tribes of the Jewish Northern Kingdom. The book of Ezra, especially chapter 9, tells how the Assyrians and other nations and faiths began infiltrating the once Jewish-only land. It was one of the strictest commands throughout the Old Testament that the Jewish nation should not intermarry with other nations, but Ezra makes it clear that the people had done just that. The offspring, known as the Samaritans, were viewed by the Jews as a mongrel breed.

As Samaritans began to fill Israel's cities, they brought their own religion and customs and mixed ethnicity. A very telling verse helps show the distress the Jews felt about this growing race: "Even while these people were worshipping the LORD, they were serving their idols. To this day their children and grandchildren continue to do as their fathers did" (2 Kings 17:41). It's not that the Samaritans abandoned the Mosaic law entirely, but they kept a watered-down version adding in other pagan religious rituals. Especially telling of the Jewish disdain for the Samaritans is that when the Jews were rebuilding Jerusalem after their Babylonian captivity, the Samaritans offered to help. Only that offer was refused. The Jews rejected the Samaritans because their genealogy was questionable. So the Samaritans, deeply offended, decided to build a temple of their own on Mount Gerizim where they could worship God.

This is key to Jesus' encounter with the Samaritan woman because when she meets Him at the well in Sychar, she asks Him, "Where is the proper place to worship? Which of the two temples is the accepted one?"

By the time of Christ's birth, the religious views of the Samaritans were closely affiliated with those of the Jews, although more like the Sadducees than the stricter Pharisees. Even more, the Samaritans rejected any doctrine not contained in the Pentateuch, the first five books of Moses. So, for example, they rejected the promise of resurrection and the belief in angels. So intense was the hatred of the Samaritans among the Pharisees that some even prayed that not one Samaritan would be raised in the resurrection. (Hardly an insult to them as they did not believe in it, but an indication of the hearts of those who did.) In one encounter with Jesus, a group of Jewish religious leaders who wished to insult and belittle Him called Him a Samaritan: "The Jews answered him, 'Aren't we right in saying that you are a Samaritan and demon-possessed?'" (John 8:48).

So, to the pure-blood Jew, the Samaritans were to be despised and avoided at all costs. This understanding only underlines the importance of Christ's compulsion to pass through Samaria: "The Pharisees heard that Jesus was gaining and baptizing more disciples than John, although in fact it was not Jesus who baptized, but his disciples. When the Lord learned of this, he left Judea and went back once more to Galilee. Now he had to go through Samaria" (John 4:1–4).

Passing through Samaria was the shortest route to get from Judea to Galilee, but it was a road that no Jew would take by choice. Instead, most Jewish people would go out of their way to avoid it. They would travel to the east and cross the Jordan River and by taking that route avoid Samaria altogether. What we have translated as "had to" in verse 4 is *dei* in the Greek, and whenever it is used in John's gospel, it means "divine necessity" or "command." In other words, it was a divine necessity and command that Jesus *had to* take that road—there was a woman who needed to know that her life mattered. Before the promise that "God causes all things to work together for good for those who have been called" was ever put down in words, Christ, the Promise, was about to bring it to a very lost soul.

> *It was a divine necessity and command that Jesus had to take [the road to Samaria]—there was a woman who needed to know that her life mattered.*

Many Jewish men then began their day by thanking God that they were not a Gentile, a slave, or a woman—and, yes, in that order. A Hebrew man would not talk to a woman on the street even if it were his own wife or daughter. Women simply weren't valued as contributors to society. There was even a sect within the Pharisees known as the "bleeding Pharisees" because they were the strictest of the strict and wouldn't even make eye contact with a woman. So if they saw that a woman was heading their way, they looked down, often resulting in walking into walls, hence their name. The fact that Jesus approached a Samaritan and that it was a Samaritan woman was shocking:

Jesus does the unthinkable

So he came to a town in Samaria called Sychar, near the plot of ground Jacob had given to his son Joseph. Jacob's well was there, and Jesus, tired as he was from the journey, sat down by the well. It was about the sixth hour. When a Samaritan woman came to draw water, Jesus said to her, "Will you give me a drink?" (His disciples had gone into the town to buy food.) (John 4:5–8)

To read this and think of how shocking this encounter was, that Christ saw beyond the barrier to a broken life, I cannot help but remember when Barry and I lived in Nashville in the late 1990s. I was a frequent shopper, so to speak, at the Humane Society. I would stop by a couple of times a week and donate supplies, take a look at all the pets, and check on which ones had been adopted. Every now and then, if there was a particularly challenged animal, malnourished or with a coat in a bad way, I would take it home and nurse it until it became more adoptable.

There was one cat, Max, that especially drew my attention. One cold night, Max had crawled under the hood of a car and onto the still-warm engine. When the owner of the car started the engine the next morning, he heard the loud cry as Max's back received an awful wound, about six inches long. The owner of the car was kind enough to bring Max to the shelter, and the vet did what he could, but Max was a sorry sight. He had no fur left on his back, and the fur on the rest of his body had been cut very short to remove the oil that had matted there, and it was now growing back at bizarre angles left and right.

"What breed of cat is Max?" I asked one day.

"I don't think Max has any dominating breed," the girl cleaning out the cages said. "I'm not sure how we'll ever get him adopted. He's a bit of everything!"

I took Max home that day.

He was one of the sweetest animals I have ever had the joy of loving. It seemed to me that his devotion came from someone seeing beyond his wounds to his wonderful heart.

Perhaps that is what is most striking about Christ's encounter with the Samaritan woman at the well: He saw beyond her culture, her gender, and even her choices. He saw a woman who was worth dying for and who would bind her heart to His, all her heart, and she would never forget that. She would see that the lonely path she had walked for so long was the one that brought her to the well that day. All the wrong choices and broken dreams had worked together to lead her to Christ, the Shelter.

64

Good Happens

It's also notable in this encounter that Jesus meets the woman when He is simply worn out. The Greek word translated as "tired" is *kopio* in biblical Greek, or *kopos* in secular Greek, which is how you would feel after being physically beaten up. In other words, Jesus is fatigued, exhausted, sore, and tired. Yet His love compels Him to keep walking when He wants to sit down, to let the crowd touch Him when He wants to be alone, and—here—to reach one woman who has made many poor choices in order to let her know that she is loved.

So as Jesus sits down, the disciples have gone into town to buy some food. That would seem reasonable to us, but it is a powerful indication that the heart and passion of Christ has already begun to impact the disciples. It was highly irregular for Jewish men to go into a Samaritan village to buy food—but Jesus sent them, so they went. He wanted to encounter this woman alone. And not only is that a remarkable thing, but add this: He spoke first.

It was unusual for a woman to be alone at the well, but perhaps her reputation was known in her village, so she came when she knew that no other women would be around. Shame is a cruel, isolating weight to bear. I remember talking to a woman at one of my conferences who said that she was very grateful we kept it dark in the auditorium. When I asked her why, she said that there would be women at the conference who knew her and would think she didn't belong.

"I had an affair," she said. "I have made so many poor choices, and now I am not welcome where I am known."

Isn't that a terrible thought, to be unwelcome where you are known?

I wonder if this was the story of the Samaritan woman, not welcome where she was known.

Jesus said to her, "Will you give me a drink?" (John 4:7).

The woman is surprised to be addressed not only by a man, but a man who is obviously a Jew.

Then Jesus, never known for small talk, goes right to the heart of the matter and of her need: "If you knew the gift of God and who it is that asks you for a drink, you would have asked him and he would have given you living water" (John 4:10).

The Hebrew word Christ uses here for "gift" is *dorea*, which means "free gift." Not only does Jesus offer a free gift, but He also tells her that the free gift is living water.

I wonder how that impacted her. Here was a woman who was probably living in a drought in her soul and spirit, just getting from one day to the next, when an unlikely stranger with a compelling gaze offers her living water. But like Nicodemus, who took Christ literally and wanted to know how a grown man could reenter his mother's womb and be born again (John 3:4), this woman wanted to know how exactly Jesus would provide this liquid refreshment when He didn't even have a bucket.

Jesus got right to the depth of her need and her story. He told her what every one of us who has ever struggled in this life before finding a relationship with Christ knows: Nothing in this world will satisfy us for long. Even the things that we believe will make us happy only do so for a moment.

The Samaritan woman knew that to be true, and Jesus was about to face her with an opportunity to come clean.

He asked her to go home and bring her husband back to the well. Interesting request.

Moment of Truth

Jesus asked the Samaritan woman to do something that she couldn't truthfully do—she wasn't married to the man she was living with. Could she tell Him that? If she told Him the truth, He might walk away with disgust in His eyes like so many had done before. He might shame her. So perhaps she should just lie and pretend that the man she was living with was her husband.

This was her moment of truth. As she looked into the eyes of Jesus, I believe she decided that, whatever the consequences, she could not lie to Him, so she told Him half of the truth: "I have no husband" (John 4:17).

Knowing that she risked a little of herself, Jesus told her that He knew the whole truth. One of the most redeeming graces of Christ is that He tells us the whole truth about ourselves without shaming us. Christ revealed that not only did He know that was true, but He knew who she was with now and how many times she had been married before.

Do you see the compelling confidence this promise offers? Christ knows all that is true about our story, the parts we own and the parts we would delete, and He invites us to bring them all into the spotlight of His grace.

> *Christ knows all that is true about our story, the parts we own and the parts we would delete, and He invites us to bring them all into the spotlight of His grace.*

The woman must have felt totally exposed, naked before this man who appeared to know her better than she knew herself. In that moment she perceived that Jesus was a prophet—for how else would He know the fine print of her life?

She had finally been exposed but in the redemptive love and grace of Jesus. Could it be that if she had never lived such a shameful life, she would not have been out alone gathering water at a time when she knew the other women would not be present?

I am not for a second suggesting that we should brazenly sin to see how God would use even that for good. What I am saying is that the very acts that Satan would use to destroy us, even those can be used by God to help us find our way home to His heart.

Good for Her and Good Through Her

What is amazing from this account is how we are shown that God not only works all things for our own good, but He also redeems our lives and works through us as well.

> *God not only works all things for our own good, but He also redeems our lives and works through us as well.*

For example, the Samaritan woman had a reputation as someone who went through man after man. After encountering Jesus she not only changed her personal life, but she was about to change others' lives. She became an evangelist to the village of Sychar! Only she must have worried that all her past, all the shame she'd borne, would affect her credibility. She knew what her reputation was and how that would affect how others viewed her. So what she did was very interesting. *What a Testimony*

She said to those who would listen, "Come, see a man who told me everything I ever did" (John 4:28). Then, rather than state, "I believe this is the Christ," she posed it as a question using the Greek word *meti*, which anticipates a negative response. It was as if she said, "This couldn't be the Christ, could it?" By planting a seed of answer in this way, she allowed the people to find out for themselves—and it's amazing what took place:

Many of the Samaritans from that town believed in him because of the woman's testimony, "He told me everything I ever did." So when the Samaritans came to him, they urged him to stay with them, and he stayed two days. And because of his words many more became believers.

They said to the woman, "We no longer believe just because of what you said; now we have heard for ourselves, and we know that this man really is the Savior of the world." (John 4:39–42)

Initially the townspeople believed because she was a changed woman. There was joy and life where there had been shame and death. They asked Jesus if He would stay for a few days, and many more believed as they sat at His feet and listened to His heart.

If we're honest with ourselves, we are all, to some degree, this Samaritan woman. Until we come face-to-face with Christ we are buried in sin and sinfulness, and He delivers us out of the oppressive story we find ourselves lost in. With the water of life He washes and refreshes us. And as the newly bathed, He sends us out with the privilege of sharing with others what we have received. This is what happened through this Samaritan woman because of Christ's commitment to graft her life into the goodness of who He is and all He intended for her.

RESTING IN THE CONFIDENT ASSURANCE THAT GOD IS IN CONTROL

This brand-new believer was given the gift of seeing that in God's hands even the worst moments of her life could bring good to herself and to those around her. Jesus didn't seek out the most reputable in the village to share Himself with. He sought out not just a woman but a Samaritan woman with a bad reputation—the lowest of the low in that culture—to show that in God's hands even the things that have broken us can be used by Him to make us whole again. There are no accidents in God's kingdom.

> *In God's hands even the things that have broken us can be used by Him to make us whole again.*

As A. W. Tozer wrote in his spiritual classic *We Travel an Appointed Way,* "To the child of God, there is no accident. He travels an appointed way."[1]

I could sit with that one truth for some time. Think about your life through that window: *there is no accident.* How does that sit with you? That might be difficult to come to terms with as there have been many moments that felt cruel or out of control. How can breast cancer or sick children or any other tragedy possibly work for good? This is a mystery that is worth wrestling with, because once we grasp the radical truth contained in this promise it will change how we view every moment of our lives.

In her beautiful devotional book *Jesus Calling*, Sarah Young uses a phrase that I love, *divine reversal*: "Joseph was a prime example of this divine reversal declaring to his brothers: You meant evil against me, but God meant it for good."[2]

If we are able by God's grace to receive the truth that every single thing in our lives will work together for good, it will transform not only how we embrace our circumstances but ultimately the purpose of our lives, which is to become more like Christ. In Romans 8:29, the apostle Paul said, "For those God foreknew he also predestined to be conformed to the likeness of his Son, that he might be the first-born among many brothers."

That is our calling: to be conformed, to be made like Christ. In this Christlikeness is our confidence.

I don't pretend to understand everything you have been through, but I do know that you are loved and cared for by a Master Refiner who never takes His eyes off you.

Through the ages those of us who meet Christ get a sense of this. I was reminded of that while reading Robert J. Morgan's book, *The Promise*, about Amy Carmichael's life as a missionary in India. One day, Amy took some children to see a goldsmith refine gold. He was sitting by a charcoal fire and had made a small crucible from two roofing tiles. Into the crucible he placed a gold nugget surrounded by salt, tamarind fruit, and burned brick dust. Every now and then he would take it out, let the gold cool a little, rub it between his fingers, then place it back in the flame and blow the fire hotter than before:

"It could not bear it so hot at first, but it can bear it now," he explained to her children.

Finally Amy asked, "How will you know when the gold is purified?"

The refiner answered, "When I can see my face in it, it is pure."[3]

All Things Work Together for Good?

When we can see God's character reflected in us, we know He has refined some of our impurities.

You may marvel, as I have, how God worked things for good in the Samaritan woman's case. But you may be wondering too, *All things, everything, work together for the good?*

71

It's a legitimate question, so let's take a look at something that happened in more modern times.

In the book *They Knew Their God*, there is a story about Samuel Logan Brengle, a leader in the early Salvation Army movement whose writings on holiness are spiritual classics. The interesting twist in Samuel's story is that he never intended to be a writer. His earliest aspirations were to be a politician, but he felt God calling him to the pastoral ministry so he enrolled in Boston Theological Seminary. A compelling speaker, Samuel wanted not only to be a good preacher but the best. He saw himself following in the footsteps of D. L. Moody, an orator of the kingdom of God. But God had other plans.

When we can see God's character reflected in us, we know He has refined some of our impurities.

Having heard the original founder of the Salvation Army, General William Booth, speak, Samuel was deeply moved by his passion for the people on the streets. And so, two days after marrying his wife, Elizabeth, they set sail for London to join the Salvation Army. General Booth was not convinced that Samuel was a good fit for the Army as he appeared a little too strong-willed and individualistic. He worked on a trial basis for six months, and his work was very menial. He polished the shoes of the other men, attended the services every night, and distributed the Salvation Army newspaper, the *War Cry*. After six months, General Booth was convinced of Samuel's call, and the Brengles returned to America as officers of the Salvation Army.

One night, as Samuel returned home from a meeting he had conducted in Boston, a drunken man who had been ejected from the meeting for disruption threw a large paving brick at Samuel's head. For some time Samuel hovered between life and death because of the blow. It took him a full eighteen months to recover. During those eighteen months he began to write. Initially he wrote articles, but they were so powerful that they were gathered together and published as the book *Helps to Holiness*. Sometime later, Elizabeth presented him with the very brick that had injured him.

On it she had written: "As for you, ye thought evil against me; but God meant it unto good, to save much people alive."[4]

This Doesn't Feel Good

There are many things in life that do not feel as if they are working together for good at all. Do you feel like the woman at the well? The drunken man? No matter who we are, I would daresay we've all done something or have become someone we believe deep down is detestable to God—because it's detestable to us.

Or what if it's something out of our control? As I was working on this chapter, I received an e-mail from a woman who wanted to know what possible good could come out of having a child with severe autism.

"No one understands," she wrote, "how heartbreaking this is or how alone I feel."

To those moments in this mother's life and to all those situations of which you are aware or are in the midst of, I would draw our hearts and attention to the earlier part of Romans 8:22–27:

> We know that the whole creation has been groaning as in the pains
> of childbirth right up to the present time. Not only so, but our-
> selves, who have the firstfruits of the Spirit, groan inwardly as we
> wait eagerly for our adoption as sons, the redemption of our bodies.
> For in this hope we were saved. But hope that is seen is no hope at

all. Who hopes for what he already has? But if we hope for what we do not yet have, we wait for it patiently.

In the same way, the Spirit helps us in our weakness. We do not know what we ought to pray for, but the Spirit himself intercedes for us with groans that words cannot express. And he who searches our hearts knows the mind of the Spirit, because the Spirit intercedes for the saints in accordance with God's will.

We live in a fallen world, a broken planet. I no longer expect anything to be the way it should be, but I take great comfort, courage, and strength from the promise that in the midst of the brokenness, the Holy Spirit intercedes for us. To my human understanding I would think that the depth of the groaning corresponds to the depth of the pain. There are times in life when words just do not come. You may find yourself in a place that is darker than you ever imagined, and you want to cry out, "How can this work out for good?"

You have a Prayer Partner in heaven, pleading for you before the throne of grace and mercy.

I want you to know that you have a Prayer Partner in heaven, pleading for you before the throne of grace and mercy. When you don't even know what to pray, the Holy Spirit does. He is God, which means He is all-powerful and all-knowing. You are not alone. When God looks upon you, He does not see a worthless thing but a gem worth ransoming and bringing into the purpose, comfort, and welcome He alone can give.

I would imagine that if we sat down with the Samaritan woman and asked her if she had her life to live over again would she make the same choices, she might say something like this: "I made many choices out of the broken places in my life. But every tear, every poor choice brought me one day closer to when I came face-to-face with Christ. For that reason alone, I would not change a moment."

As you reflect on your life, I pray that you can say with absolute confidence that although there have been many turns in the road, God used every bend to bring you under the shelter of who He is.

Judy's sister
Mary's brother-in-law
Liz's nephews (family)
(Marilyn mother) — Virginia fever
Kathy's mother
  Potassium low
40 — nephew Jason - alcoholic
      kidney - salvation

5

LOVE

I Don't Believe That Anyone Could Really Love Me

THE PROMISE

For I am convinced that neither death nor life, neither angels nor demons, neither the present nor the future, nor any powers, neither height nor depth, nor anything else in all creation, will be able to separate us from the love of God that is in Christ Jesus our Lord.

—ROMANS 8:38–39

When I came to America in the 1980s, one of my favorite radio personalities was Paul Harvey. There was something about his voice that I found so soothing, like a grandfather who would sit down by the fire, eyes sparkling, and draw you into the story he was telling. Whether it was the reassuring statement, "In times like these, it helps to recall that there have always been times like these," or his signature sign-off line, "I'm Paul Harvey. Good day!" I smiled and felt a little better about the day ahead. When he died in 2009, he was ninety years old. If you look at his Web site, www.paulharvey.com, all that remains is the following statement:

A great tree has fallen, and left an empty place against the sky . . .

Of all the stories that Paul told over his seven decades in broadcasting, I don't think any has impacted me more than a story he told on Christmas Day 1965. As I sat in church one Sunday morning, the pastor played a recording of Paul and his story "The Man and the Birds." This is what I remember:

It was Christmas Eve, and a man told his wife and children that he didn't intend to go to the midnight service with them. He explained to them that the whole idea of God becoming a baby was just too much for him to believe, and he would rather stay home. Not long after the family left, it began to snow. As he watched out the window the snow flurries got heavier and heavier, so he settled into his armchair by the fire to keep warm.

A few minutes later he heard a thump on his window, then another and another. Assuming that it was neighborhood children throwing snowballs at the window he peered outside, but what he saw surprised him. He saw a flock of birds huddled together in the snow. He realized that they must have been trying to evade the storm and, seeing the lights on in his house, flew into his window by mistake. He knew that if he left them in the snow they would die, so he decided to open the door to the barn where his children kept their pony. He wrapped up in warm clothes and boots and trudged through the snow, opened the barn door, and put the light on to draw their attention, but the birds wouldn't come. He went back to the house and got some bread and left a trail from as close to the birds as he could get right up to the barn door, but still they wouldn't come. He tried to catch them, but they were so afraid that they scattered in all directions.

It was clear to him that the birds were terrified of this large creature approaching them through the snow. They didn't recognize him; they didn't trust him, and they didn't understand that he wanted to help them. Every time he tried to touch them, they moved farther and farther away from help.

If only I could be a bird for a moment, he thought. Then I could tell them not to be afraid and speak to them in their language. Then I could show them the way to the safe, warm barn. But I would have to be one of them so they could see and hear and understand.

Just then the church bells began to ring out—"Adeste Fideles."

> *Oh, come, all ye faithful,*
> *Joyful and triumphant!*
> *Oh, come ye, oh, come ye to Bethlehem;*
> *Come and behold him*
> *Born the king of angels:*
> *Oh, come, let us adore him,*
> *Oh, come, let us adore him,*
> *Oh, come, let us adore him,*
> *Christ the Lord.*

> *Yea, Lord, we greet thee,*
> *Born this happy morning;*
> *Jesus, to thee be all glory given!*
> *Word of the Father,*
> *Now in flesh appearing!*
> *Oh, come, let us adore him,*
> *Oh, come, let us adore him,*
> *Oh, come, let us adore him,*
> *Christ the Lord.*

As the sound washed over him, he dropped to his knees in the snow. Love had changed everything.

THE PROMISE OF RELENTLESS LOVE

That is the promise God offers us in Romans 8:38, and not just in a slight way, but with relentless pursuit and unshakable devotion. What an unspeakable gift that God would come to us in Christ, in human flesh with the voice of a baby, to show us the love that is in His heart for us. Not only did He come as a baby, but He poured out His life for us to secure, for now and for all eternity, that nothing can separate us from the love of God. Nothing, not time or circumstances or space. He loves us for keeps and tells us: *I belong to you and you belong to Me—forever.* What a comfort that declaration is for every wounding moment you feel cast away, unloved, and unwanted. What peace and joy that brings to the life that has been shunned. A promise like that could make the lonely, despairing soul dare to reach out to the world again. A promise like that shatters walls of isolation and ushers in enough love to be passed around.

He loves us for keeps and tells us: **I belong to you, and you belong to Me—forever.**

That's exactly how such a promise affected one woman I know. Only she didn't just reach out for hope. She grabbed onto it with her very life.

Looking for Love

For twelve years this woman, unnamed in the Gospels, had been tortured, whispered about, and avoided. She was an outcast because of a condition that caused her to hemorrhage. In Jewish culture, this condition required a bleeding woman to be deemed unclean, avoided, and ostracized. For twelve years, then, this woman had no belonging, no community, no love, or even a kind touch. She was shunned and forced into isolation. She had not been able to attend worship in the temple or visit with friends over dinner, because any dish she touched or chair she sat on would be ritually unclean. If she had been married, she would now have been cut off from her husband and all her family. Here is her story of loneliness and anguish:

> When Jesus had again crossed over by boat to the other side of the lake, a large crowd gathered around him while he was by the lake. Then one of the synagogue rulers, named Jairus, came there. Seeing Jesus, he fell at his feet and pleaded earnestly with him, "My little daughter is dying. Please come and put your hands on her so that she will be healed and live." So Jesus went with him.
>
> A large crowd followed and pressed around him. And a woman was there who had been subject to bleeding for twelve years. She had suffered a great deal under the care of many doctors and had spent all she had, yet instead of getting better she grew worse. When she heard about Jesus, she came up behind him in the crowd and touched his cloak, because she thought, "If I just touch his clothes, I will be healed." Immediately her bleeding stopped and she felt in her body that she was freed from her suffering. (Mark 5:21–29)

This account comes right after the Gadarenes begged Jesus to leave after the shocking exorcism, so He and the disciples got back on the boat and sailed back to the western shore of Galilee. It seems as if during Jesus' three-year ministry, people either welcomed Him with open arms or begged Him to leave. His presence always evoked a powerful response, and it would be no different back in Capernaum.

Now in Capernaum, a crowd waits for Him. Though everyone there is eager to see Jesus, there are two people who have a desperate need for a miracle. One is this woman. The other is Jairus, a Jewish religious official, ruler of the synagogue in Capernaum, a man whose daughter is critically ill.

Jairus begs Jesus to come and touch his daughter so that she will be healed.

Jesus goes off with Jairus, even though the people keep following and, in fact, begin to press in on Him. And that is where Jesus stops in His tracks.

Someone in the crowd reaches out and grabs hold of a miracle— and Jesus feels it.

"Who touched me?" He asks.

Hundreds of eyes, the bewildered faces of the crowd of people pressing on Him, stare blankly. Though everyone's leaning into Jesus, everyone denies that they touched Him.

Peter asks the Lord—and you can almost hear the incredulity in his words (only recorded in Luke 8:45): "Master, the people are crowding and pressing against you." *Everyone's touching You, Lord. Who isn't trying to touch You?*

The disciples completely miss it. They don't understand that miracles cost Christ dearly. He *felt* power leave Him. No, that's not it, Jesus says. "Someone touched me; I know that power has gone out from me" (Luke 8:46). Only Jesus is acutely aware of what has happened in this moment: Jesus and the one who touched Him—the hemorrhaging woman.

Take a closer look at her and what this event meant. Touching even the hem of Jesus' robe, which is what she did, was no small thing. It meant a huge risk for this woman. Under Old Testament Law:

> When a woman has a discharge of blood for many days at a time other than her monthly period or has a discharge that continues beyond her period, she will be unclean as long as she has the discharge, just as in the days of her period. Any bed she lies on while her discharge continues will be unclean, as is her bed during her monthly period, and anything she sits on will be unclean, as during her period. Whoever touches them will be unclean; he must wash his clothes and bathe with water, and he will be unclean till evening. (Leviticus 15:25–27)

The Bible doesn't tell us why this woman was hemorrhaging. We can only presume the possibilities: Did she have fibroid tumors? A hormone imbalance? An infection for which there was no cure at that time? Imagine: this woman had lived under the banner "unclean" for twelve years. She wasn't just away from people for seven days, but twelve years plus seven days.

Mark, in his Gospel account of this story, describes her condition as an affliction. The Greek word used here is *mastigos*, which translates literally as "scourge." When this word is used, it combines two elements: extreme physical suffering and shame.

This was a woman in pain in both body and soul.

Physically, she had no doubt lost weight and even strength. She must have been dangerously anemic. Financially, she was ruined. Mark tells us she had suffered a great deal under the care of many doctors. She had tried anything to make a difference. The Gospels corroborate that she had spent every cent she had seeking help, but no treatment or diagnosis or regimen worked. In fact, Mark says, she was worse than when she began.

Have you ever been that desperate?

I have a friend who discovered that the birth of her child brought on multiple sclerosis. Her life changed almost overnight. She went from being a bright, bubbly woman, full of energy and life, to one whose body betrayed her a little more with every passing month. She went from doctor to doctor, trying what traditional medicine offered, and even nontraditional medicine and treatments. She even subjected her body to being treated by bee stings, several sessions in fact, to see if the regimen would work. It was incredibly painful, and in the end it made no difference at all.

The hemorrhaging woman of the Gospels was like this, shattered, isolated, in complete despair. Today she might have found a support group. Then, she was a pariah. Other than Mary, the Magdalene, who was delivered by Jesus from seven demons (Luke 8:2), I don't think there is a more wretched woman in the whole New Testament. And yet, though she had no love, she had not given up hope that, at a divinely appointed moment, it would be within arm's reach.

Love Makes You Take Risks

Capernaum and all the villages around Galilee are abuzz with the news of the miracles of Jesus. Everywhere He goes, people are being healed, restored to new lives of purpose and joy. The hemorrhaging woman hears the news and runs to the seashore that day, hoping for her own miracle, waiting for even a glimpse of this amazing Jesus. Something about desperation stokes these fires, the lingering embers of what-if and if-only.

If only I touch His clothes, I will be healed, the hemorrhaging woman thinks (Mark 5:28). She holds onto the hope that Jesus can do what no one else, no legion of doctors, could do.

But there is such a large crowd around Jesus, and she will have to move through the very people who, for more than a decade, have called her unclean and untouchable. Everyone is trying to gain a better place to see Jesus, to be close to Him, even that prominent man, Jairus. And Jesus is stopping to listen to Jairus, agreeing to go with him.

What can I do? she wonders.

The woman pauses. She has no rights here. She shouldn't even be here. She is unclean, untouchable. Anyone or anything who touches her will also be unclean, untouchable for at least seven days. Plus, she can't ask Jesus to help her before He goes to the house of Capernaum's lead rabbi, whose twelve-year-old daughter was dying! She was the antitheses of Jairus's daughter, who was loved, fought for, treasured, her whole life ahead of her. No one fought for this woman anymore. She had no champion.

Have you ever been there? Are you there right now? Perhaps you learned a long time ago that fairy tales are cruel in their promises because no one came to the rescue.

But the possibility of love, transforming, healing love, is too great. The woman makes a life-changing decision. No matter what this costs her, how can her situation be any worse? She has spent everything already anyway: her finances, her very self. In effect, she is a walking dead woman.

Her crossroads makes me think of one very low point in my own life. A friend had said to me, "When the pain of staying the same is greater than the pain of change, then you will change." *desperate*

That simple but profound statement stuck with me and comes to mind now. At times, the place where we are, even if painful, can be familiar and give us a sick sort of comfort. Have you ever been in a place where you knew God was calling you to step out and grasp hold of life, but it was just too scary?

The hemorrhaging woman was in this place. She faced the possibility of public humiliation and sanctioning by the crowd and, worse, by the rabbi and Christ Himself. She knew that the moment she touched Jesus, she would make Him unclean. If He were ritually unclean for the next seven days, He would not be able to enter Jairus's home. Would her desire to be whole cost this child her life? Regardless of the consequence, how could she go on like this when a possibility for change was *right there*?

Not Worth Saving

You would think this woman's struggle with her social standing and loneliness would be enough torture, not to mention the options she's weighing between her health and a child's life. But can you imagine what kind of mental and emotional anguish must have entrenched itself inside her heart and mind? Just as the demons ripped at the poor man living among the dead, the hemorrhaging woman has been wrestling with her own demons of self-hatred, tapes on repeat in her head for *twelve years*.

You know these lies. We have all heard them before, and especially at those moments when God calls to us to take a risk and love as He loves:

Who do you think you are?
You will never change!
There is no hope for you.
If people knew who you really are, no one would want you.
Why do you keep trying? Things will never change.
You are worthless!

One of the enemy's greatest strategies is to make us believe that we are not worth saving and not worth loving. He will torment us with his evil accusations. But the thing we can remind one another of, that no one was there to remind this woman of that day, is this: Satan is not omniscient. Unlike our Father, who knows our thoughts before we think them, the enemy does not. The songs of David remind us of this:

> O Lord, you have searched me
>   and you know me.
> You know when I sit and when I rise;
>   you perceive my thoughts from afar.
> You discern my going out and my lying down;
>   you are familiar with all my ways.
> Before a word is on my tongue
>   you know it completely, O Lord. (Psalm 139:1–4)

This is key to understanding God's promise to love us. He gives us tools to believe and risk and hang on to Him. Satan can whisper a lie to you, but he has no control over whether you will believe it. The love of Christ knows no boundaries, recognizes no labels. Some cultures exalt men over women, but Jesus does not. Some nations hold up the white man over the black man, but Jesus sees beyond skin color with a love that penetrates any prejudice. Whatever there is in your life that makes you feel separate—whether it's the label "divorced," "childless," "sick," "unemployed," "mentally ill"—the apostle Paul speaks to that place, saying that nothing in all creation will be able to separate us from the love of God in Christ Jesus our Lord.

The love of Christ knows no boundaries, recognizes no labels.

Of course there are things in this life that press in on us like that crowd, threatening to distance us from God and His love. You can fall back, but you can try exercising the faith of the hemorrhaging woman too.

Try this. In those hard moments, when you're questioning God's love for you, think of yourself as standing at the top of a flight of stairs. You hear that first lie: *God doesn't care. There's no hope.* If you choose to let that lie seep into you, then you move down another stair. As you buy in deeper and deeper to the lies and the despair, your steps gather momentum until you find yourself tumbling to the bottom in a defeated heap.

If you reject the first lie, though, the enemy cannot bring you down. The trouble is that his lies are so subtle at first and feed into how so many of us already feel about ourselves, like a familiar tape that plays over and over in your head, telling you negative things you have heard for years.

You can stop the tape. It's not a onetime thing, but you can start replacing every lie with God's Word, His promises, reaching out to the hem of Jesus' robe. Jesus is the eternal place of promise, the place where a miracle can happen—because for every problem, there is a promise.

> *Jesus is the eternal place of promise, the place where a miracle can happen—because for every problem, there is a promise.*

The problem: *"I am overwhelmed with anxiety!"*
The promise (Philippians 4:6–7): "Do not be anxious about anything, but in everything, by prayer and petition, with

thanksgiving, present your requests to God. And the peace of God, which transcends all understanding, will guard your hearts and your minds in Christ Jesus."

The problem: *"No one sees how much I have to carry!"*

The promise (Matthew 11:28): "Come to me, all you who are weary and burdened, and I will give you rest."

The enemy would love to make us trip and fall and never get close to Christ, who is cloaked in the promise of God's love. But we get to choose whether we buy into the enemy's lies or not. He counts on the fact that this strategy has worked before, but by God's grace, we can change that. And a woman no one believed in and had been pushed aside is about to show us how.

FROM DESPAIR TO DAUGHTER

I am amazed that this broken, physically weak woman, who may have walked for up to thirty miles to get to Capernaum, kept moving. Once Jairus had begged Christ to come to his house, there must have been a shift in momentum, an urgency now in the pace of Christ and His followers as they headed to where a little girl lay dying.

The woman must have groaned as her chance of healing was moving double-time through the streets of Capernaum. Her moment of opportunity was slipping away as Jesus moved through the crowd.

But she rallies. She chooses to believe there *only* still is hope. With every ounce of strength left in her body she pushes through and reaches out to grab the hem of Christ's garment. A touch is all she can muster. Even a touch is all she needs, even a fleeting touch of love, when you have been unloved and untouchable for so long. So when she sees a small gap in the crowd, she reaches out and touches the hem of Jesus' robe. "Immediately her bleeding stopped and she felt in her body that she was freed from her suffering" (Mark 5:29). The word translated "edge" is Greek *kraspedon*, meaning "edge, border, hem of a garment." But it can also refer to the tassel that Israelites wore on the four corners of the cloak. Why did she reach out to the hem of His cloak and not touch His arm or His hand? It would seem that all she had the strength left to do was to reach out and touch the last part of Christ as He walked away. As she knelt in the dirt and the dust kicked up by a clamoring crowd, she took the last vestiges of hope and spent them on one touch.

The hemorrhaging stopped. Just like that. Did she sense it straightaway? Can you imagine what that must have been like? She lived with the wind of shame blowing in her face for year after year, and in a moment, the wind simply stopped. The pain disappeared. She was clean. She was revived. Instead of her life's blood flowing out of her, new life and power coursed through her veins.

How easily this woman could have slipped back into the crowd, privately elated by the miracle, content in knowing she had received just what was needed. There's indication that she was going to take the healing and go on her way—she didn't cry out or exclaim; she didn't even try to stop Jesus and thank Him.

But Jesus doesn't give us what we *believe* we need. He gives what He *knows* we need, and He gives it out of love for us, deep, undeniable love. Jesus wanted this woman who had lived so long in isolation, unloved, untouched, to receive not just resolve of her affliction, but a relationship with Him that would change everything. And a restoration with her family and community. "At once Jesus realized that power had gone out from him. He turned around in the crowd and asked, 'Who touched my clothes?'" (Mark 5:30).

> *Jesus doesn't give us what we believe we need.*
> *He gives what He knows we need, and He gives*
> *it out of love for us, deep, undeniable love.*

TELL YOUR STORY

The disciples thought this was one of the most ridiculous questions that Jesus had ever asked. The crowd was pushing against Jesus, jostling to get a better view. Children would be playing at His feet, and no doubt Jairus would be almost running, ushering Jesus along at a fast pace. What did Jesus mean, "Who touched my clothes?"

But Jesus knew. He felt it. He felt the power of God flow from Him. And He didn't ask the question because He didn't know the answer or because He wanted to be thanked or wanted to humiliate the woman in front of the crowd. He asked because He loved her so. He wanted to give her so much more than she knew to ask for—she wanted to be healed in her body, but Jesus wanted her to be healed in her mind, spirit, and relationships too.

It's interesting that the Hebrew word for "salvation" is *sozo* and means "to be saved" and "to be healed, to be made whole." If the hemorrhaging woman had crept away that day, would she have wondered if she had stolen a miracle? Did she know that Jesus already knew who she was and that there would be no judgment on her condition, only healing? Notice though that Jesus didn't point her out when she touched Him and say, "It was you, wasn't it?" He let her decide whether she would step out or not: "Then the woman, knowing what had happened to her, came and fell at his feet and, trembling with fear, told him the whole truth" (Mark 5:33).

THE WHOLE TRUTH

What an amazing gift Christ gave this woman. He gave her a place to tell Him all that was true, and in that most vulnerable moment, a chance to be fully seen and fully loved.

Have you ever told Jesus the whole truth? Scary thought to some of us, yet the great irony is that He already knows all that is true and loves us anyway. If the woman had slipped away that day, her body might have been healed, but would residual shame be her new ongoing affliction?

Instead, this brave, broken, healed woman fell at Jesus' feet and told Him everything. We don't know what she said, but I imagine she told Him how her affliction started and what it had cost her. She told Him of how alone she had been for so long. She told Him about the shame and the pain and the fear. Perhaps she hoped for mercy, but she got much more: "He said to her, 'Daughter, your faith has healed you. Go in peace and be freed from your suffering'" (Mark 5:34).

This is the only time in Scripture when Christ addressed one woman as "daughter."[1] Such a tender, inclusive greeting to someone who had been an outcast for so long! Everyone around Christ that day heard Jesus speak these words. He declared that it was her faith that had brought her healing and wholeness, and then He sent her off with a prayer of blessing and peace.

We never get to meet her again in Scripture, but I wonder what the rest of that day was like. If she was married, she had not been able to touch her husband's hand in twelve years, or kiss her mother's cheek, or sit around the table with friends laughing and discussing life over a good meal. In my mind's eye, I see her eventual return to her family, her approach to her house. If the seven-day waiting period still held true, even after the miracle, the family surely would have heard about her healing. Did they know their long-lost mother was coming home?

Maybe they were milling about the house, the dad, the children, cleaning up after a meal when the door opened slowly, about to reveal a life touched by His love.

WHAT ABOUT JAIRUS'S DAUGHTER?

As wonderful as this healing and restoration is, if I were Jairus, I would have been completely unconcerned. Maybe I would have been annoyed or even angry. His dying daughter is his only care. Running is all that is on his mind at this point, getting to the house. He is consumed with urgency. His heart is beating out of his chest. Every second that Jesus spends here, taking time to hear this hemorrhaging woman's story, means another second that his daughter is closer to death. And then the word comes: "'Your daughter is dead,' they said. 'Why bother the teacher any more?'" (Mark 5:35).

Jairus must have been ready to cry out, but Jesus hears the proclamation and turns to the synagogue official and says, "Don't be afraid, just believe" (Mark 5:36).

Then leaving the crowd and allowing only Peter and James and John (James's brother) to accompany Him, Jesus goes to Jairus's house. Maybe He knew there was already quite a crowd there, weeping and wailing in a mourning dirge. Jesus looks at the frenzied grief, and you have to see the love and compassion in His eyes. He offers words to calm the grieving people, to give them peace. "Why all this commotion and wailing?" He says. "The child is not dead but asleep" (Mark 5:39).

The people laugh at Jesus. But Jesus doesn't have time to entertain the crowd. He puts out everyone from the house except Jairus and his wife, and Peter, James, and John. *This is no place*, Jesus' actions tell us, *for laughter or mockery or disbelief*. He goes to where the little girl is and takes her by the hand. "Little girl, I say to you, get up!" (Mark 5:41).

Straightaway the little girl gets up and begins to walk around.

WHAT KIND OF LOVE IS THIS?

I find it interesting that Jairus's daughter is *twelve* years old.

Think about the parallels of this day. For twelve years the hemorrhaging woman suffered and struggled, was broken and sidelined. For twelve years, Jairus had loved his little girl. I wonder if Jairus sat that night and reflected on the strange "coincidence," as some might call it, that for every day of his daughter's life, this woman had been in pain. When his little girl learned to crawl, the woman was in pain. When his little girl took her first step, the woman was suffering. When his little girl was old enough to spend the night at her best friend's house, this woman was still crying out in the darkness.

This was no coincidence and illustrates so clearly two things about God and His promise to love us. First, your status in life makes no difference to God's love for you. Christ treats every person, whether child or aged, afflicted or dead, with a dignity that our world does not. He did not say to the woman, "I'd love to hear your story—after I take care of this important man's daughter." No, He took all the time she needed right there and then.

The second thing is a greater mystery. Jairus's little girl was only allowed to struggle for a short time before Christ healed her, but the hemorrhaging woman had to wait twelve years.

What kind of love is that? some might ask.

Can anyone answer? A girl died and was quickly brought back to life. A woman suffered many years and was eventually brought back to complete health. Was one trial worse than the other? Was one state more horrible than the next?

One sort of trial and pain cannot be deemed more severe or

horrible than the other. Pain is pain, whether it's a girl's or a woman's. Suffering is suffering, whether it hurts for a short time or years. Loss is loss, whether it takes away something for a moment or a lifetime. There are some things on this earth that we will never understand. But the love that heals all, transforms all, and brings life to all—it is the same. The love that made Jesus give the untouchable woman not only physical healing but spiritual and emotional wholeness also pulled a dead child by the hand from the grip of death. His love longs to touch every life and allow it to reach into Him as well.

So let me ask you a question: how long have you been bleeding? Very few of us will ever know the kind of physical loss of blood that this woman faced, but how long have you been bleeding from shame or a wound so deep that you believe it will never heal? I invite you to come back to the feet of Christ and, this time, tell Him your whole story.

For neither death nor life, nor angels nor rulers, nor things present nor things to come, nor powers, nor height nor depth, nor anything else in all creation, will be able to separate us from the love of God in Christ Jesus our Lord.

Kathy Dale

Clef Stein
Auston
Lisa – allergy (Kathy Ex -friend)
Russell – Camera – throat
Marie – pain scoriosis
Jerilyn – meds prayers

6

GRACE

I Have Failed

The Promise

My grace is sufficient for you, for my power is made perfect in weakness.

—2 Corinthians 12:9

I will never forget the funeral for Eleanor, my mother-in-law. This was the first time I ever saw the body of someone who had died. When I was growing up in Scotland, the funeral director would collect the body, and the family wouldn't see it again until the casket was sealed. Eleanor died of the ravages of colon cancer that spread to her liver. In her late sixties, she was a relatively young woman.

In the last days of her life, she had asked if I would do a couple of things for her after she died and before her body would be viewed by those who came to pay their respects, since paying respects is a very big deal in her hometown of Charleston, South Carolina. She asked if I would be the first to see her and make sure that she looked like she wanted. She asked if I would check her hair and put on her the earrings that I wore on my wedding day. She also asked if I would put around her neck the necklace that Christian used to bite on when he was teething, and if I would tuck into the casket her favorite picture of her with Christian.

For those of you who are more familiar with this side of life-and-death ritual, these things may not seem enormous, but for me they were overwhelming. I was very nervous at the prospect, but it was important to her, and I couldn't say no.

Five of us went to the funeral parlor that day. Barry, his dad, and I were joined by our dearest friends, Mary Graham and Ney Bailey. The funeral director, who was a family friend, showed us into the room where the casket rested on a table at one end. Everyone hung back for a moment. Then with earrings, necklace, and photo in hand, I moved forward.

A china doll, I thought. That is exactly how Eleanor appeared to me. Her hair and makeup looked right, and there was a kind of elegance about her still features. Elegance may sound like a strange word to use, but Eleanor was always, like me, quite a talker and lived up to the stereotypes of her fiery red hair, only now she seemed almost poised, serene.

It was only as I bent over to put on the first earring and my hand brushed her cold, waxy cheek that the reality of it all hit me. I put the other earring on her other ear, added the necklace, and pinned the photograph of Eleanor and Christian onto the satin pillow on the casket lid. As I moved a piece of her hair to where I knew she wore it, the last conversation I had with her played in my mind.

"Sheila," she asked, "I know we have talked about this before, but do you really believe that God loves me as much as He loves you?"

"With all my heart I do," I said.

"I'm not so sure. Don't you think He must love some more than others? The good ones, the ones who give Him all their lives, the ones who don't make so many mistakes?"

"Mom, God's love for us is based on who He is, not how we act," I said. Even as I said that I thought of one of Eleanor's favorite expressions, "Straighten up and act right!"

"Mom, I know that for most of your life you have believed that God's love is based on whether we make good choices or bad choices, but the cross makes it pretty clear that no amount of good choices would ever be enough. You are loved just the same on the days when you feel you've done a good job as on the days when you know that you have blown it."

"I know you believe that," she whispered. "It's just hard to hold on to."

You are loved just the same on the days when you feel you've done a good job as on the days when you know that you have blown it.

THE PROMISE OF GRACE

Eleanor was right. It is hard to believe that God loves each of us equally, without measure or merit, and that His grace shelters us regardless of what we do or leave undone. I think it's so hard because there is no other relationship on earth like that. Every other relationship we have is affected, to some extent, by how we behave and what we say.

In a friendship, if we abuse that relationship in any way, there are consequences. We become more distant and formal. At times, if our behavior is inappropriate enough, it will cost us that friend. For the child who yells, screams, or refuses to listen to a parent, there's a cause and effect. In marriage, a couple stands before God, family, and friends to vow love to one another until death parts them. Yet about half of all marriages end in divorce because of our behavior and choices. Every earthly relationship proves to us that love and acceptance is conditional, and we can mess it up at a moment's notice.

That's why being loved forever based on nothing but someone else's ability to love unconditionally is, as Eleanor said, "hard to hold on to." Doesn't each of us struggle to believe in such love, such grace? Don't we each find that earthly love fails us, both intentionally and, as in death or tragic separations, unintentionally?

As I was working on this chapter, I took a break for a snack and turned on the television. The show *Family Feud* came on. I don't know if you've ever seen this game show, but the basic premise is that there are two families competing to win a cash prize. They are asked a question like, "Name one thing you purchase without trying on." Both teams have to come up with the most popular answers given by one hundred people surveyed. As I sat down with my cheese and crackers, the question was, "Name one thing a man changes when he makes a lot of money." I almost choked when I realized that the number one answer was, "His wife!" No wonder we struggle to accept God's unconditional love. The only place that we find love like this is in the heart of God our Father and expressed on this earth through Christ, His Son. That kind of divine love is grace.

When you think of the word *grace*, what comes to your mind?

I always heard grace described as "unmerited favor." The Old Testament concept of grace could be described that way, too, but adds some other ideas that can be a little confusing. For instance, the oldest, most reliable Greek translation of the Old Testament, called the Septuagint, translates "grace" as "favor"—for example, "Noah found favor in the eyes of the LORD" (Genesis 6:8). And then the same word for grace is used in Genesis 32:5, where Jacob steals the birthright from his brother, Esau, and sends gifts, he says, "in order that I may find favor in your eyes." So it's clear that favor was shown to Noah because of how he lived, but then there's Jacob, and the idea of forgiveness is planted because he sought favor from Esau for a grievance. Add to these two ideas one more: look at God's dealings with the children of Israel, and you'll see His grace defined as "mercy" and "favor" displayed over and again as the Israelites rebel and turn away from Him. One example is when Moses strikes a rock twice instead of speaking to it as God has instructed him—Moses is not allowed to enter into the promised land of Canaan for his misdeed (Numbers 20).

In the New Testament, a fresh wave of grace bursts upon us. In the Greek, the word for "grace" is translated *charis*, from which we get the word *charity*, also meaning "love," "goodwill," and "loving-kindness." To participate in this grace, this unmerited favor, the only requirement is a relationship with Jesus Christ:

> Consequently, just as the result of one trespass was condemnation for all men, so also the result of one act of righteousness was justification that brings life for all men. For just as through the disobedience of the one man the many were made sinners, so also through the obedience of the one man the many will be made righteous.
>
> The law was added so that the trespass might increase. But where sin increased, grace increased all the more. (Romans 5:18–20)

Paul emphasizes this in talking to the Romans. The grace of God, he says, is free but never to be seen as a license to sin: "What shall we say, then? Shall we go on sinning so that grace may increase? By no means! We died to sin; how can we live in it any longer?" (Romans 6:1–2). So, on one hand, we have this gift that we can never earn or pay back; and on the other, we are called into relationship, where the closer we get to God's heart, the more like Him we become and the less we want to sin.

It sounds complicated, doesn't it? Yet one thing is crystal clear: God is always the initiator of this love and mercy—of the kind of strength that fills in our weaknesses, the kind of perfection that covers our flaws, and the kind of shelter that says, "I'm going to keep you and love you through all your failings." God is the one who pursues us, who woos us to this place of grace, to the shelter of His promises.

God is the one who pursues us, who woos us to this place of grace, to the shelter of His promises.

My thirteen-year-old son defines this kind of grace as "forgiveness." When I asked him to explain, he said, "Well, when you think that He is God and we are not, there is no reason for Him to keep loving us when we mess up. But He does. He forgives us. That is grace."

Yes, that is grace.

Where we mess up, He mends it. Where we are weak, He is strong. Where we struggle with imperfections, He rushes in to touch us and lovingly shows us the way He sees us and calls us to be. He patiently listens to our doubts and fears and proclaims, *With all My heart, I'm telling you that you are loved just the same on the days when you feel you've done a good job as on the days when you know that you have blown it. You are loved and always will be loved, and I am going to love you and forgive you to the very end.*

102

THE EXTENT OF GRACE

Jesus emphasized this truth, God's pursuit of us, in story after story that He told through His ministry. Nearly every illustration He gave was to remind us of the heart of God and the extent to which grace will go to reach us. Three of His parables, in particular, are clear about failings and where God comes in to fill the gap—about things or people who were lost: the lost sheep, the lost coin, and the lost son. In each story, the theme is consistent: the lost cannot restore anything—and do not need to (Luke 15).

In the story of the lost sheep, the shepherd who had one hundred sheep leaves the ninety-nine to go and look for the one that is lost. When he finds it, rather than scold the sheep, he puts it on his shoulders and brings it home, inviting his neighbors to rejoice with him that he has found this precious lamb.

In the story of the lost coin, a woman had ten coins, Greek drachmas, each worth about one day's wages. When she realizes that she has lost one, she lights a lamp and sweeps the entire house until she finds it. When she does, she invites all those in her community to celebrate with her that what was once missing is now found.

But the prodigal son is perhaps the most moving, and to the hearers it was the most controversial of all. Here grace is presented in its most stark and arresting form:

> "There was a man who had two sons. The younger one said to his father, 'Father, give me my share of the estate.' So he divided his property between them.
>
> "Not long after that, the younger son got together all he had, set off for a distant country and there squandered his wealth in wild living. After he had spent everything, there was a severe famine in that whole country, and he began to be in need. So he went and

hired himself out to a citizen of that country, who sent him to his fields to feed pigs. He longed to fill his stomach with the pods that the pigs were eating, but no one gave him anything.

"When he came to his senses, he said, 'How many of my father's hired men have food to spare, and here I am starving to death! I will set out and go back to my father and say to him: Father, I have sinned against heaven and against you. I am no longer worthy to be called your son; make me like one of your hired men.' So he got up and went to his father." (Luke 15:11–20)

Most of us are familiar with this story—so familiar, in fact, that we fail to realize how shocking it was to those who heard it live from Jesus' lips. In part, maybe that's because we live in a culture bombarded by reality television and talk shows that survive on the heartache and poor choices of dysfunctional families. Even within Christian circles, it's not so unusual to hear of a child who decides to reject the standards of the family and head out to "find" him- or herself. But to the crowd who heard the story that day, it would be a tale of the greatest shame that could be brought on a family. The culture was very much a patriarchal society, and respect and honor for the father was an unspoken mandate. Every element that Christ included in the parable only added to the shock value:

- *A boy insults his father by demanding his inheritance before his father is even dead. This would be deeply offensive to those listening to the story.*
- *To increase the insult, the son heads for the big city and wastes the money that his father had worked so hard to secure, on one wild party after another.*
- *When the son is finally destitute and scouring through the very food he is feeding the pigs (an unclean animal to the Jews, so to even be in their presence was an affront), he decides to return home and beg for a job on*

his father's estate. By rights, he should never show his face to his father again.

As the crowd listened to Jesus tell the story, they must have anticipated hearing what retribution the father would exact upon the son. I can see the people looking at one another, shaking their heads in horror that such a thing could happen! It's one thing for a dumb sheep to get lost; one might search for that since it's property. And the coin? One would look for a day's wages. But wait expectantly for a son who has spoken a death wish to his father then dares to return for any kind of mercy at all? Unthinkable.

No one in the crowd that day would be prepared for what Jesus presents as the outcome of the story:

"But while he was still a long way off, his father saw him and was filled with compassion for him; he ran to his son, threw his arms around him and kissed him.

"The son said to him, 'Father, I have sinned against heaven and against you. I am no longer worthy to be called your son.'

"But the father said to his servants, 'Quick! Bring the best robe and put it on him. Put a ring on his finger and sandals on his feet. Bring the fattened calf and kill it. Let's have a feast and celebrate. For this son of mine was dead and is alive again; he was lost and is found.' So they began to celebrate." (Luke 15:20–24)

A Party for Sinners

As far as the listeners were concerned, the prodigal son's father should have written off the boy. Instead, he was watching for him every day, waiting, hoping this might be the day he would come home. So many aspects of the story seemed outrageous: that this ungrateful and defiant son was worth everything to the father and that the father would run to greet this son when he did return home (how undignified for the patriarch of a family ever to be seen running, yet this father was running to the very one who had defiled his dignity). Truly outrageous. There was no precedent for this kind of love and mercy, for this kind of grace.

The prodigal son had prepared some kind of speech as he trudged the hot weary miles home, but he never got a chance to get it all out, for the father was already yelling instructions to the servants: "Bring the best robe in the house, put a ring on his finger as a sign that he is a beloved son, not a servant, and whatever animal we have been saving for a rainy day, kill it now for grace is raining down!"

"This is outrageous!" the people listening to Jesus might have said.

That was the whole point. The love that God has for us is unprecedented, outrageous, and overwhelming, especially for one man in the crowd that day who heard the story. Even though he had heard it, he had no idea how much he would need the truth of those words in days to come.

The love that God has for us is unprecedented, outrageous, and overwhelming.

As I have walked through this story that I have known since I was a child, I have found myself in unexpected places: I am the prodigal, and I am the elder brother. Christ's masterful art of storytelling is like a mirror held up for us to see if we will see. That would be deeply offensive to the listening crowd that day, for in effect Christ was saying, "See yourself here. You are the central characters." Each of us in our own way has squandered what our Father has given us, perhaps not as blatantly as the younger son, but in our own way. Don't you think each of us has felt a surge of self-righteous indignation as God's grace had welcomed back one who has offended us at a core level, not just to the fold but to a party? Grace is offensive before it is liberating.

A Promise for Peter

It was amazing that Peter would be near Jesus to hear any of these parables, let alone the one of the prodigal son. Peter, after all, was not the type to sit in the synagogue or at the feet of the teachers and scribes and listen. Even as the story fell on his ears, he would have no frame of reference to understand how deeply this story of failure and redemption would become his life song.

Peter began his life as a fisherman in Bethsaida (John 1:44). Nathaniel and Philip, two other disciples of Jesus, were from the same village that lay on the shores of upper Galilee, and they all worked together. Peter's fishing business had obviously prospered because by the time we meet him in the Gospels, he had moved to Capernaum, the leading city of Galilee, and had gone into partnership with James and John, two other members of the Twelve.

Archaeologists have uncovered what they believe to be the remains of Peter's house in Capernaum, and his property was fairly large.[2] For some reason I have always had a picture in my mind of a simple man who went fishing every day with his friends, but it's clear that Peter was a successful businessman who ran quite a fishing empire. One day he met a man who changed everything:

> As Jesus was walking beside the Sea of Galilee, he saw two brothers, Simon called Peter and his brother Andrew. They were casting a net into the lake, for they were fishermen. "Come, follow me," Jesus said, "and I will make you fishers of men." At once they left their nets and followed him. (Matthew 4:18–20)

What was it about Jesus that compelled Peter and Andrew to drop what they were doing and go after Him? I believe that they were called into mission with Jesus and felt it deeply. I'm sure at that stage they had no idea what the day ahead would hold, never mind the coming weeks and months, but they felt the call of God and responded.

The role of disciple was not an unknown role in those days; it had a clear job description. A person in those times enrolled not in a seminary but as a student of an established rabbi. They would literally live with their master and learn by listening and asking questions. The goal was that the disciple would become like his teacher. Jesus described it like this in Luke 6:40: "A student is not above his teacher, but everyone who is fully trained will be like his teacher."

So the goal was clear: not just to learn from Christ but to become like Christ.

The goal was clear: not just to learn from Christ but to become like Christ.

It seems apparent that the other eleven men looked on Peter as the leader. Anytime the disciples are listed, Peter is always listed first. Even when it is the three men who are Christ's closest friends, Peter is always named before James and John. It is more than that, though. Peter obviously had a special relationship with Christ. On one occasion early in their friendship, Jesus asked Peter to pull his boat out into deep water in the morning and put down his nets. Peter was a veteran fisherman who knew to fish at night in these waters, but because Jesus asked him to do it, he did. When the nets began to fill to breaking point with fish, his response to Jesus was to ask Him to leave: "Go away from me, Lord; I am a sinful man!" (Luke 5:8).

Could it be that Peter was more aware of his own flawed humanity in the presence of Christ's holiness than we have supposed over the ages? Certainly Peter was compelled by the Lord's perfection and his own imperfection. For example, remember the night the disciples spent in a boat, trying to get across the Sea of Galilee in a fierce storm?

Remember the evening after Christ fed five thousand men. Exhausted from that and heartbroken by the news of the execution of John the Baptist, Jesus sent the disciples on without Him while He headed to the hills to be alone with His Father. The disciples were having a hard time making any headway against the wind that was whipping the sea into a frenzy. At about three o'clock in the morning, they became aware of a figure approaching them walking on the surface of the waves. Initially they were terrified, but Jesus called out and identified Himself.

Peter was the one who spoke up:

> "Lord, if it's you," Peter replied, "tell me to come to you on the water."
>
> "Come," he said.
>
> Then Peter got down out of the boat, walked on the water and came toward Jesus. But when he saw the wind, he was afraid and, beginning to sink, cried out, "Lord, save me!" (Matthew 14:28–30)

I think Peter gets a bit of a bad rap. We talk about his lack of faith, but he was the only one willing to get out of the boat at all. Peter's character seems to have been a bit impetuous, loud at times, but fiercely loyal too. The harsh reality that Peter was going to have to face is that our ways are not God's ways, and God's grace is made perfect in our weakness, not in what we perceive as our strength.

This is one of the greatest ironies of our faith: at the moment when we realize we have nothing to give Christ and we fall flat on our faces, we bring the gift He has been asking for all along. That gift is our hearts—not our ideas or skills or preferences. Just ourselves.

> *This is one of the greatest ironies of our faith: at the moment when we realize we have nothing to give Christ and we fall flat on our faces, we bring the gift He has been asking for all along.*

Sometimes, however, it takes the failure of all we believe that we bring to Him to bring us to this truth. Sometimes it means coming to the table with nothing in order to enter the very heart of Christ.

A FINAL MEAL

When the disciples gathered with Jesus to celebrate the Passover feast, they sat around the table eating together. Luke's gospel tells us that Jesus addressed Peter:

> "Simon, Simon, Satan has asked to sift you as wheat. But I have prayed for you, Simon, that your faith may not fail. And when you have turned back, strengthen your brothers." But he replied, "Lord, I am ready to go with you to prison and to death." Jesus answered, "I tell you, Peter, before the rooster crows today, you will deny three times that you know me." (Luke 22:31–34)

What a strange passage. There are some mysteries of faith whose meanings are hidden from us. Why would Satan be allowed to mess

110

with Christ's followers? What is it about the process of pain and failure and disappointment and disillusionment that in God's hands becomes polishing cloths for our grimy hearts?

I told a friend recently that I was writing about Peter and how through his failure he discovered the beauty of grace. She wrote right back: "Well, I just hate that! Why does it always have to be so hard?"

I smiled at her response.

I understand, don't you? In the end, Peter surely did, and the words of Christ from their last supper probably came back to him— maybe with regret at first and then with piercing love.

It's at that Last Supper that Jesus says to Peter, "Satan has asked to sift you as wheat" (Luke 22:31). Interestingly, the word used for *you* is plural. Christ is telling Peter that Satan has asked to sift them all (all the disciples), but Jesus goes on to say that He has prayed for Peter—"you"—singular.

What a gift to Peter that Jesus has prayed for him, not believing that he won't fail but rather knowing that he *will* fail and that He, our Maker, is praying for when Peter turns back so he can strengthen the others. Peter will never understand grace until he has tasted bitterly of failure, but that very failure will be the path that will lead him to finding his strength and shelter in Christ.

Do you see the wonder in that? The Lord is making it clear to Peter that his failure will not disqualify him from being the leader Christ knows him to be and that He, the Lord Himself, is praying for Peter!

It is easy in hindsight to see that as a gift, but not for Peter, who was in the middle of this drama that was about to play out in a brutal fashion, out of his control. When Jesus told Peter that before the cock crowed he would deny Him, Peter was adamant that he would go to prison or die before abandoning Christ.

I believe that Peter meant that with all his heart, but he was going

111

to discover that though his spirit was willing, his flesh was weak, and that God's ways are not our ways.

Don't Lie Down Like a Lamb

When Jesus and the disciples leave the room after their meal, they walk down to the Mount of Olives. When they came to the garden, Jesus takes Peter, James, and John in farther with Him to pray. The disciples try to stay awake with Jesus, but sleep overcomes them. Perhaps the meal and the wine or just the exhaustion of the previous few days take over, but though they want to be there for Jesus, they cannot help themselves.

That is when chaos breaks loose. A crowd of men rushes into the garden: soldiers, officers from the chief priests, Pharisees; they're all brandishing torches, lanterns, and weapons that light up the night. Peter rises to his feet, pulling his sword from its sheath, and strikes out. He is doing all that he knows to do to stand with Christ, no matter what it cost him, even if it means his life this night.

So when Jesus tells him to put away his sword, Peter is shocked. Jesus predicted just hours earlier that Peter would deny Him, and yet here Peter is, ready to fight to the death for His Master. *What's wrong with Jesus? Why isn't He fighting, and why is He stopping His defense?*

Peter must have been so confused. Can't you almost hear him thinking, *Lord, I will fight for You, but don't expect me to just lie down like a lamb and take it!*

So when the Romans arrest Jesus and lead Him away, Peter follows at a distance. Evil is in the air, hatred and all the powers of darkness. As Peter stands in the courtyard of the high priests, he is recognized—not once, not twice, but three times. Each time, he denies knowing the prisoner.

As dawn begins to break, a cock crows and everything that is important to Peter, all he thought he brought to the table, is shattered in the morning light.

The Promise amid the Mess

We don't know what happened to Peter in the hours between his denial and the moment when he heard, after the crucifixion, that the tomb was empty. He and the other disciples must have felt wretched and lonely. If you have built your whole life on being strong, a man of your word, a leader, and then when it counted most, you failed, where do you go?

If you have taken your father's inheritance, broken his heart, spent all you had, and end up feeding pigs, where do you go?

If you're a fiery redhead who believes that God loves those who are quiet and hold their tongue and you've struggled until it's too late, where do you go?

Peter would tell you, the prodigal would say, Eleanor would urge you: turn your heart toward home, toward God, to His promise that He's got you covered with His lavish, unmerited grace. His power is made perfect in your weakness. We recognize our need of the Shelter when we stand exposed and vulnerable.

See what happens next.

It is very early on the morning after the Sabbath, after Jesus' murder, and Mary Magdalene, Mary the mother of James, and Salome come to the tomb to anoint Christ's body.

But the tomb is empty. Jesus' body is gone. There is an angel present and he's terrifying, but he has a message. First, he calms the women. "Don't be alarmed," he says (Mark 16:6–7). But they are alarmed. And they are shocked because the angel tells them that Christ has risen and He is going before them to Galilee. The angel says, "He has risen! He is not here. See the place where they laid him. But go, tell his disciples and Peter, 'He is going ahead of you into Galilee. There you will see him, just as he told you.'"

And Peter.

Do you hear the grace poured out here in two little words, words that will mean everything to the hotheaded disciple who feels he's messed up one time too many? Do you hear God's messenger making it clear: *Make sure the one who thinks that he has failed knows that Jesus is waiting for him.*

The promise that was Peter's and Eleanor's and the prodigal's is yours as well: "My grace is sufficient for you, for my power is made perfect in weakness" (2 Corinthians 12:9).

When Paul wrote, "My grace is sufficient," he wrote it in the present tense. He was saying right now, at this very moment, whatever you are facing—God's grace is enough. Unlike his opponents who wanted to see miracles as a sign that God was with Paul, he turned that upside down and said, "No, it's in my very weakness that God shines, and His strength holds me."

It's tempting to long for miracles and great power in our Christian walk to show that God is with us and loves us, but the kingdom of God is no sideshow or three-ring circus. Rather, God is glorified when in our weakness we lean on His strength.

Do you feel that you have failed, that you are washed up, unsaveable, unloved? Then join the throng of us who, when we expected to be put in our place, instead found a robe around our shoulders, a ring on our fingers, and a party thrown to celebrate that a heart that felt lost has been found. This is the glorious, outrageous way of the kingdom of God that calls us to take another look in the mirror after we have fallen and failed. We brought all we had, and not only was it not enough, but it tripped us up and sent us running into the night feeling abandoned and alone.

But if you will listen for a moment, you will hear the music that pierces our shame and calls to the party all who are weak to find their strength in God alone. Grace doesn't tell us that our bad choices or failures don't matter; quite the reverse. Grace tells us that our failures expose us for who we really are, and even as we are ready to count ourselves out, the shelter of the cross casts its shadow over our broken hearts and welcomes us home.

Russell & Marie
Susan - prayer for family
Karen Bussard - auto immune disorter
Judy's sister - June 2nd port for Cance
    Ilona - new.
Cliff
Mary - Auston death

(1) We suffer because we live in fallen
    World II Cor 4: 7-10
(2) We suffer because God uses it to produce
    good in us; James 1: 2-4
(3) suffering prepares us for how
    God will us us II 1: 3-9
(4) suffering teaches us that this
    world is not our final home.
        II 2 Cor. 4: 16 - 5:5

June 1

7

HOPE

I'm Broken

THE PROMISE

God has said, "Never will I leave you; never will I forsake you." So we say with confidence, "The Lord is my helper; I will not be afraid."

—HEBREWS 13:5–6

When I was sixteen years old, I believed that my calling in life was to be a missionary and to come home with stories of the amazing things God was doing in remote and unfamiliar territory. This quest was inspired at an early age by the Baptist Missionary Society (BMS), and a little green plastic bank in the shape of a globe that sat on the bureau in our living room. Every week my mom would add a few coins to the bank, and when it was full, she would send it off to the BMS. For a time, she served as the missionary secretary in our church, and I loved to hear her stories of what was happening overseas. I think underneath it all, I wanted to take some hope to places where hope seemed scarce. When you have walked through any kind of tragedy as a child (as I had with the loss of my father), it can tenderize your heart and propel you to reach out to others who have walked or are walking in dark places.

I loved that as a family we were involved in helping others overseas, but there was one thing that made absolutely no sense to me. At church we regularly knitted woolen squares for blankets to send to Africa. As far as I could tell from television specials or *National Geographic* magazine, it was hot in Africa. Why were we knitting blankets for children there? And why were we encouraged by the BMS headquarters in Glasgow, Scotland, to use bright, primary colors? Who came up with the notion, anyway, that these children liked stripes? I never did get answers to these questions, and we continued to produce squares in the most headache-inducing combinations of colors known to mankind. I couldn't see any self-respecting African children wanting to wrap themselves in these garishly colored blankets. Still, we kept on knitting as if the future of world evangelism depended upon it.

What I did love was how every now and then a missionary would be home on furlough, a leave of absence from the mission field for a few weeks. I loved their visits and had a romanticized idea of their lives both here and there. Of course, I knew that furloughs weren't much of a break as missionaries had to spend most of their time traveling from church to church, telling stories of their experiences and raising financial support before going back into the field once more. But I loved the stories and the slides showing that the missionaries were working with people to find help and hope. Sometimes, however, they found a little more than that, more than they or I had bargained for.

One particular missionary story and slide show stands out in my mind. First, you must know that our church had a box for ongoing donations of clothing for anyone in need. Some of those would be sent to our missionaries in Africa. This was a huge gift to me. One could place any item there that one's mother wanted one to wear and which one detested. The way I saw it, this was sort of like practicing tithing, only with clothes, because it just happened that I had a white, fluffy bolero jacket-cardigan thing that I hated, but my mom insisted I keep. The jacket had been expensive, she said, so I should be grateful. Finding it hard to muster gratitude, I decided instead to donate the bolero to some poor, unsuspecting child in Africa. If the children there liked the striped blankets we had been making, they would love this jacket. I hid it deep in the box and forgot all about it.

When this particular missionary visited our church, she talked for a little while about the people and her work in the villages. Then she showed some slides of the children. I will never forget the shock that silenced me as onscreen flashed a photo of a little girl wearing nothing but my white bolero jacket!

"A miracle!" I declared after several moments.

My mother was not so convinced.

Fluffy boleros and garishly colored woolen blankets aside, the fact was I had romanticized the idea of the life of a missionary. As with any rose-tinted image of life, however, my childhood picture of the mission field was not even close to reality.

THE PROMISE OF HIS PRESENCE

Isn't that the way of life? You have beautiful visions of what can be and expectations of how things should go. Then life gets hard. Losses threaten to strip you of hope rather than cover you with increased faith. People leave you, rather than come bearing gifts and good news.

Suffering sits down, takes you firmly by the hand, and gives you a slide show of your life, and you're left feeling more alone in darkness than ever.

How does God's promise to never leave us or forsake us—to be our helper—fit into this picture? Is His promise about as relevant as just another striped woolen blanket sent into a sun-baked land?

Believe me, I have wondered. Even now one of my greatest challenges in sharing my faith is a passionate commitment to tell the truth about God's promises, but also about how hard life can be and how difficult it is at times to believe. Every day so many of us wrestle with these contrary feelings:

> *I know that Jesus is the Way, but I feel lost.*
> *I know that He is my Healer, but I'm struggling with sickness.*
> *I know that all things work together for good to those who love God and*
>   *are called according to His purpose, but I'm just not seeing how certain*
>   *things can.*
> *I know that Christ promises peace, but I'm anxious and frenzied.*

Our experiences with pain and struggle, trouble and hardship do not diminish the promises of God at all. Nor do we, however, need to enhance those promises. This is important because too often in evangelical circles we seem obliged to act as if we are God's PR agents. We're confronted with a hard reality, and God's promise to help us, to never leave, suddenly feels false. Yet we pretend otherwise. We smile and say things are okay. We profess that the promises must be true, when in our hearts we're angry and confused, hurt and feeling more alone than ever, because how could we think such things? How could we feel this way?

The truth is, God doesn't want us to pretend our faith or give lip service to His promises. No, He calls us to live with questions draped in assurance. Or, as my friend Randy Elrod says, God wants us to "be restless on the journey and confident in the destination."[1]

God doesn't want us to pretend our faith or give lip service to His promises.

This is the picture of a true child of God, whether in your own neighborhood or overseas. Dr. Helen Roseveare showed me this.

In the hardest circumstances, the most wrenching of events, Helen's life shows that God's promise of hope and comfort is real and true. Helen, born in England in 1925, was highly educated, having attended a prestigious all-girls school when she was just twelve years old, and then Cambridge, where she became a Christian. Her family attended church when she was a child, but she credits those she met through Christian Union at college with helping her understand the gospel for the first time. She was impassioned to become a missionary, so she focused on finishing her medical degree to use her skills and knowledge helping those most in need. At age twenty-eight, she set sail for the Belgian Congo (now known as the Democratic Republic of the Congo) with Worldwide Evangelical Crusade (WEC).

However, the rose-tinted horizon that Helen saw quickly darkened. In her book *Give Me This Mountain,* she tells of immediate resistance to her efforts to train the locals in health care and how men at the mission post failed to give her, a young single woman, any respect. This led to a lot of frustration and at times anger.[2] These things, however, would be the least of her worries, as no training or linguistics program could have prepared her for what she would face one day in 1964:

"It was a Saturday afternoon," recalls Roseveare. "A truck drove into the village where I lived, and I could hear the noise from house of rough, angry voices shouting. And then two men burst into my home. That was the first indication I had that we were at war. [The men] inspected everything and smashed a lot of my property, and then I suddenly realized that they were intent on evil. I tried to run away and hide, and they came with powerful torches, and they found me. They struck me, they beat me. I lost my back teeth to the boot of a rebel soldier that night. They broke my glasses. I can't focus on anything if I haven't got them on. That was most frightening. When you can see them, you can at least put an arm up to take the blow. When you can't see, you're so defenseless." During the course of the evening, Roseveare was badly violated by her perpetrators. "I don't think I was praying; I was numb with horror, dread, fear. If I had prayed, I think I would have prayed, 'My God, my God, why hast thou forsaken me?' I felt He'd left me. I didn't doubt God. I never doubted God. But I felt, for that moment, that He'd left me to handle the situation by myself."[3]

Have you ever been there? Have you walked through a situation so painful and lonely that it seems as if you are on your own? Perhaps you have a chronically sick child, and with each rushed visit to the emergency room, you wonder if God is there or if you have to get through this one by yourself. Or you are fighting to hold together your marriage, doing all you can, but it doesn't seem as if God is doing much to support you.

Many men and women in Scripture felt that way.

- *Gideon replied, "if the LORD is with us, why has all this happened to us? Where are all his wonders that our fathers told us about when they said, 'Did not the LORD bring us out of Egypt?' But now the LORD has abandoned us and put us into the hand of Midian" (Judges 6:13).*

- *Job cried out, "Why did I not perish at birth, and die as I came from the womb?" (Job 3:11).*
- *David pleaded, "Why, O LORD, do you stand far off? Why do you hide yourself in times of trouble?" (Psalm 10:1). And, "My God, my God, why have you forsaken me? Why are you so far from saving me, so far from the words of my groaning? O my God, I cry out by day, but you do not answer, by night, and am not silent" (Psalm 22:1–2).*
- *Even Christ on the cross, cried loudly in pain, echoing part of Psalm 22, "Eloi, Eloi, lama sabachthani?"—which means, 'My God, my God, why have you forsaken me?'" (Mark 15:34).*

The experience of walking through a dark night is a common bond for those who love God. The redemptive element in this struggle is the ability to turn to those coming behind you and let them know they are not alone. There is a comfort that only the One who has walked through the night into the morning can bring that comfort to another still in the darkness.

So it was for Dr. Helen Roseveare, who was held captive by rebel forces for five months with other missionaries. She was such a bearer of light when she went on to write how God used her brutal rapes to bring comfort to other single women missionaries. Some of these women feared, since they had lost their virginity due to a rape, that they might have lost their salvation too. Helen knew otherwise. She knew that even in rape, her relationship with God had not been damaged. She had not failed God in any way. For these women who suffered, it was only because of what Helen had been through that her words held such weight.

The comfort she gave others out of her own pain and trauma makes me think of one of my favorite passages of Scripture:

> Praise be to the God and Father of our Lord Jesus Christ, the Father of compassion and the God of all comfort, who comforts us in all our troubles, so that we can comfort those in any trouble with the comfort we ourselves have received from God. For just as the sufferings of Christ flow over into our lives, so also through Christ our comfort overflows. If we are distressed, it is for your comfort and salvation; if we are comforted, it is for your comfort, which produces in you patient endurance of the same sufferings we suffer. And our hope for you is firm, because we know that just as you share in our sufferings, so also you share in our comfort. (2 Corinthians 1:3–7)

Suffering and comfort, after all, are companions who walk hand in hand. Comfort hovers for suffering to appear, and suffering demands that comfort be present. For us God has both covered: He is the God who suffers with us, one arm embracing suffering, and He is the God who brings comfort to us, the other arm with care and understanding and His very Self.

That idea has changed my understanding of the promises of Christ. We are promised by God: "Never will I leave you; never will I forsake you" (Hebrews 13:5). The Scripture doesn't say we will never hurt, but rather that we will never be alone in that hurt. We can be sure to say, then, "The Lord is my helper; I will not be afraid" (Hebrews 13:6).

My friend Evelyn Husband told me how this became clearer to her after her husband's death. Rick was the commander of the space shuttle *Columbia*, which exploded upon reentry into Earth's atmosphere on February 1, 2003. Evelyn told me that although she has loved Psalm 23 since she was a child, she had never really understood verse 4: "Even though I walk through the valley of the shadow of death, I will fear no evil, for you are with me; your rod and your staff, they comfort me."

At Rick's memorial service, this psalm was read, and someone pointed out that for there to be a shadow, there must be light. Christ, whom John 1:4 tells us is the Light of the world, entered the shadows so that we wouldn't have to ourselves. He experienced the dark for us so that we never would be alone.

God's promises are so much greater than our feelings. They are sound and sure, the stuff to nail your heart to in the worst travails of life. Dr. Helen Roseveare shows us that even when you don't feel God's presence, you can be assured He is there and find His comfort and hope. Another woman who walked with Jesus wrestled with what seemed to be an absent God. She struggled to find comfort when He transformed her life and then disappeared, even though she refused to leave Him. But she is a woman who learned that God is there even when you don't feel Him, and sometimes, when you least expect it but most need it, believing can mean seeing.

God is there.

LOOKING FOR HOPE

If ever there was a woman who needed God's presence and Christ's comfort, it was Mary, the Magdalene. Now there has been a lot of misunderstanding as to which Mary the Mary of Magdala was. Some Bible readers suggest she was the sinner who anointed Jesus' feet and wiped them with her hair as He reclined at the home of Simon the Pharisee (Luke 7:36–50). But Scripture does not support that.[4] Other Bible readers say Mary is the woman caught in the act of adultery in John 8, but there is nothing in the biblical canon that supports that or the notion that she was a prostitute either.

What we do know, when we first meet her in Luke's gospel (Luke 8:1–3), is that Mary Magdalene has been a tormented soul. She is traveling with Jesus, the disciples, and other women whom Christ had touched, after being healed of many demons. She was possessed by not just one, but seven demons when she meets Jesus somewhere along the shores of the Sea of Galilee. We know that she comes from a noble family and that her hometown is Magdala, on the northwest shore of the Sea of Galilee. But we don't know details of her healing or her face-to-face encounter with Jesus, just that He banished the powers of darkness from her life:

> After this, Jesus traveled about from one town and village to another, proclaiming the good news of the kingdom of God. The Twelve were with him, and also some women who had been cured of evil spirits and diseases: Mary (called Magdalene) from whom seven demons had come out; Joanna the wife of Cuza, the manager of Herod's household; Susanna; and many others. These women were helping to support them out of their own means. (Luke 8:1–3)

And maybe that is enough: to have been brought from such a dark life into one of light and peace. Would that not change everything, would that not make you want to linger with the source of that light, chase it, dwell in it the rest of your days?

That may be why it's indicated that Mary's wealthy family may be underwriting the ministry of Jesus. With their coins and riches, they affirm the comfort and hope Christ gives.

I am sure that for Mary Magdalene and the other women who underwrite Christ's work, what they gain cannot compare with what they can give.

When heaven invades your hell, it wins your heart's allegiance.

When heaven invades your hell, it wins your heart's allegiance.

That truth must be what draws Mary to the cross. We do not see her again in the Gospels until the crucifixion, burial, and resurrection of Christ—and she is not only there but also figures prominently in the account. Near the cross of Jesus, Mary stands with His mother, His mother's sister, and Mary the wife of Clopas (John 19:25).

I am not a feminist, but I think it notable and interesting that the ones who never left Jesus during those murder scenes were the women. Perhaps they knew that they were not in as much danger from Jewish authorities, who would discount their presence for they were only women. Whatever the reason, they were there, and I have often wondered what Christ's cry, "My God, my God, why have you forsaken me?" did to them, in particular to Mary Magdalene.

Jesus made seven statements from the cross, three of them before a strange darkness covered the earth at noon. When the darkness fell, there was silence. Christ, who had known no sin, became sin for us (2 Corinthians 5:21). He was abandoned, alone, as even His Father had to turn away. Of the seven cries from the cross, the fourth was the most passionate and desolate. Christ quoted from Psalm 22 as He alone bore the sin of the world. Even in our darkest moments, we will never know the depth of all Christ endured so that we will never have to be alone. He cried out for comfort, but no comfort came. Yet, even in this unspeakable spiritual torture, the cry was personal: "My God, my God." Mary Magdalene heard it all.

I mean, _she was there_. She stayed by Jesus through the persecution and at the cross. She followed His body to the grave and even there she lingered. She had seen comfort and felt hope and both resided in

Jesus' eyes. So, surely, when Jesus uttered that heartrending cry from the cross, no one would understand that desolation more than Mary Magdalene. As she watched Him struggle and writhe in pain, His cry had to be like a dagger in her heart.

And the twist, the final stab? When He cried out, "It is finished."

IT'S OVER WHEN GOD SAYS IT'S OVER

The Jewish authorities who had plotted to have Christ crucified now intended to make sure that all rumors died with Jesus. By assigning an official military guard to the site where the slain Jesus was entombed, the powerful Jewish Sanhedrin had a round-the-clock watch at the burial place. Afraid that the disciples might remove the body, and thus give credence to Jesus' remarks about a resurrection, the Jewish Council took care from the very first moments of Jesus' burial to guarantee that the grave site remained secure and sealed.

But we read in Matthew's gospel that an earthquake thrust open the tomb, and the sleeping soldiers were faced with the unthinkable reality that Jesus' body was missing.

> There was a violent earthquake, for an angel of the Lord came down from heaven and, going to the tomb, rolled back the stone and sat on it. His appearance was like lightning, and his clothes were white as snow. The guards were so afraid of him that they shook and became like dead men. (Matthew 28:2–4)

The guards passed out from sheer terror, which was just as well as this moment did not belong to them. This moment had been planned for Mary the Magdalene before she was even born.

Night turned to morning, then before morning broke on the

third day, Mary hurried to the tomb to anoint Christ's body. He had been buried quickly to get it to a place of rest before sundown on the Sabbath, and now Mary wanted to take care of it according to custom:

> Early on the first day of the week, while it was still dark, Mary
> Magdalene went to the tomb and saw that the stone had been
> removed from the entrance. So she came running to Simon Peter
> and the other disciple, the one Jesus loved, and said, "They have
> taken the Lord out of the tomb, and we don't know where they have
> put him!" (John 20:1–2)

Mary was horrified and told Peter and John that someone had taken Christ's body. She assumed it must have been His enemies. When Peter and John looked inside the tomb, they saw that it was empty and the grave clothes were wrapped and lying there. They believed and went home, the Scriptures say (John 20:8–10).

Mary Magdalene did not.

She wept and bent over to look into the tomb and saw two angels in white, seated where Jesus' body had been. One angel is at the head of the place, and the other at the foot. They asked her, "Woman, why are you crying?"

> "They have taken my Lord away," she said, "and I don't know
> where they have put him." At this, she turned around and saw Jesus
> standing there, but she did not realize that it was Jesus.
>
> "Woman," he said, "why are you crying? Who is it you are
> looking for?"
>
> Thinking he was the gardener, she said, "Sir, if you have carried
> him away, tell me where you have put him, and I will get him."
>
> Jesus said to her, "Mary."

She turned toward him and cried out in Aramaic, "Rabboni!" (which means Teacher). (John 20:13–16)

There is nothing more beautiful than your name on the lips of the one you love. How much more so to hear Christ utter your name when you thought you had lost Him forever. They all did. Peter, James, John—they left everything behind to follow Christ, and as quickly as He had entered their lives and changed them forever, He was gone. How could they return to business as usual when Jesus had turned everything that used to mean something into nothing more than existing? Now only one would be given the gift of hearing His voice again for the first time since His brutal execution. How gracious of Jesus to save this moment for Mary Magdalene, this first sighting by any man, woman, or child of His resurrected body. Mary, who had been tormented by the demons of hell, would receive a gift of not just believing but seeing the victorious Christ.

Suffering and comfort go hand in hand indeed, and in having been to hell and back, Christ and Mary share this beautiful moment—the kind of moment Christ longs to share with each of us. He had defeated darkness once and for all, and He allowed the one who had been there, too, to celebrate the moment with Him first.

So we hold on to this promise that God has given us: He will never leave us, never forsake us. Christ embraced all of death's leaving and forsaking for us so that we need never be alone. Even in the darkest night, He is there. Christ brings life from death. Nothing you are walking through is taken lightly by your Father. He will use it to bring comfort and healing to another broken heart. You can be sure when you say, "I will not be afraid because the Lord is my Helper." Time after time, I have heard the same thing from women who have walked through devastating times: "I would never have signed up for this, but I know Christ now at a depth and with an intimacy that I never knew was possible." The hope Christ promises becomes more real because of the trial.

We hold on to this promise that God has given us: He will never leave us, never forsake us.

Ask Dr. Helen Roseveare. Ask Mary Magdalene. You could certainly ask me, and I would tell you: He is light, the glory of God. He is grace, this amazing gift. He is the Cleft in the Rock into which you can retreat when broken and weary. You will find understanding in His shelter, and you will find hope in His presence because He will wrap His arms around yours. He will hold your faint heart with His nail-scarred hands. He will be there, always, an infinite comfort and hope.

Connor - should be fine
Jerilyn - vacation with
          family.

Mary - testimony + husband

Marie - tues, CT
          Wed. Russell - test cancer
          Thurs   "   phone visit
          Fri.   Marie Dr report
Shelly - feeling better, healing
Julie - daughter exhausted
Clif Stine - passed away.
Jerilyn - Connie

8

STRENGTH

I Feel Things Are Crashing Around Me

THE PROMISE

In this world you will have trouble. But take heart! I have overcome the world.

—JOHN 16:33

I first met Joni Eareckson Tada (she was just Joni Eareckson then) in 1983 at a Christian festival in Holland. On the surface, we looked very different. There was the most obvious, that Joni was in a wheelchair, having broken her neck in a diving accident as a teenager. But there was much more too: Joni looked elegant and poised in a lovely silk blouse, tailored pants, and silk scarf, with her blonde hair blown into a beautiful style that framed her face. I wore jeans and a leather jacket, and my hair was short, black and purple, and spiky. We looked like Junior League meets rock and roll.

Differences in appearance didn't matter, though, when we looked into each other's eyes and talked for a while. We knew we would be friends. We may have looked different on the outside, but we saw what matters most to us much the same way. I don't know if you have ever had the joy of meeting Joni or reading any of her books, but there is a gentle, strong grace that lives inside her. She smiles a lot and loves to sing, which she did at that festival in Holland. We shared a love for the same things and saw each other off and on throughout the next few years at conferences or conventions, always looking for ways to grab even a few moments to catch up on each other's lives.

Over the years, I often wondered what Joni's day-to-day life was really like, how much she suffered quietly. To look at her warm smile and well-groomed appearance, you would assume this spirit came easily, but Joni is disarmingly honest in telling us that it does not. She describes an encounter with a group of women she met in a restroom at a woman's conference where she had been speaking.

One woman, putting on lipstick, said, "Oh, Joni, you always look so together, so happy in your wheelchair. I wish I had your joy!" Several women around her nodded. "How do you do it?" she asked as she capped her lipstick.

I glanced at the nicely dressed women around me. I knew that the break would soon be over. How could I answer her question in 60 seconds? How could I sum up in a sound bite what has taken me three decades of quadriplegia to learn?

"I don't do it," I said. That raised their eyebrows. "In fact, may I tell you honestly how I woke up this morning?" Several women leaned against the counter to listen. "This is an average day." I breathed deeply. "After my husband, Ken, leaves for work at 6:00 a.m., I'm alone until I hear the front door open at 7:00 a.m. That's when a friend arrives to get me up.

"While I listen to her make coffee, I pray, 'Oh, Lord, my friend will soon give me a bath, get me dressed, sit me up in my chair, brush my hair and teeth, and send me out the door. I don't have the strength to face this routine one more time. I have no resources. I don't have a smile to take into the day. But you do. May I have yours? God, I need you desperately.'"[1]

One of the great sadnesses and ironies of Joni's life is that even though she is paralyzed from the neck down, she still suffers considerable pain. You would think that paralysis means an absence of pain, that you feel nothing, but Joni has not been given that relief. The strength that I always see in her is not a timid thing. It has been and continues to be a brutal battle each day to celebrate Christ in the midst of her reality. Yet each day she relentlessly puts on her internal boxing gloves and fights.

When I interviewed Joni on *The 700 Club* television show in 1991, I became even more aware of a dimension in her relationship with Jesus, an iron core of strength that was both intangible and yet undeniably real. At the time, I couldn't have told you then what this dimension was—was it endurance? Resilience? I wasn't exactly sure. I just know I wanted it. I wanted to know what she knew. I wanted the relationship she had with Christ that was obviously not borne out of an easy life. Clearly, Joni had lived a life of suffering. Was suffering the key, the thing that birthed this quality that I couldn't quite define?

I did not want the suffering—who does?—but I did want the knowing that she possessed, and the strength.

So when I said good-bye to Joni that first day we met, I determined to stay in touch and grow our friendship. Then in 1992, my life fell apart and I lost touch with everyone.

THE PROMISE OF STRENGTH

I sat in the psychiatrist's office in the hospital, and I could hear him talking to me, but it was as if I was listening through glass or trapped inside a goldfish bowl. His eyes were kind, and his posture as he leaned forward seemed to invite trust, but I was done with that. He talked to me about recent developments in understanding clinical depression and new medications that were more efficient in arresting that crushing feeling of disappearing a little bit more each day. I could tell that he was offering me hope, but I wasn't taking it.

It's not that I saw him as anything other than the fine doctor he proved to be. I just wasn't interested. He offered the first few steps on a path to recovery and wellness, and I didn't want it. The *drip, drip, drip* of depression had taken its toll until I finally felt as if I were drowning and had no strength or desire left to fight. I felt as if I was going under, as John Keats describes: "I am in that temper that if I were under water I would scarcely kick to come to the top."[2] Even though this doctor was throwing me a life preserver, I didn't have the energy or desire to grab hold of it.

I find it strange now as I sit at my kitchen table, typing these words, to step back into that place of utter darkness and despair. It seems like another life. I watch my thirteen-year-old son throwing a football with his dad out the window and marvel that, at one point, I wanted to die.

I have written and talked about my experience with depression through the years, and I have known an instant connection with others who are suffering or have suffered. We don't need many words there—just an understanding of how dark that night can be.

A friend recently suggested that I should see this as part of my past and not talk about it anymore: "After all, you don't want to be the poster child for depression, do you?"

I'm not sure. Perhaps I do. Not in the way of being stuck in the past and unable to get on with my life, but certainly in being present and available for those just beginning their descent. Depression is a very isolating disease, which only adds to the despair. I want others to know what I discovered, that there is help and healing available, that one day again you will actually want community and crave not just the company of others but closeness too. It doesn't happen overnight, but every step in the right direction lifts the darkness just a little.

In the days and weeks that followed the beginning of my treatment, I can only describe it as being aware of the faintest glimmer of light. "Unless the LORD had given me help, I would soon have dwelt in the silence of death. When I said, 'My foot is slipping,' your love, O LORD, supported me. When anxiety was great within me, your consolation brought joy to my soul" (Psalm 94:17–19).

There is something holy that God has tucked into suffering. I wouldn't even attempt to say what suffering might look like or feel like for you at this moment. But let me say that as I fell off the edge of my life, I discovered that I had always been held. In some mysterious way, it was as if God reached out and grabbed hold of me and lifted me. I was physically weak and emotionally worn out, but aware of the beginnings of that something that I had seen deep in Joni's eyes, that oneness with Jesus. Initially I wanted to run from the powerlessness of dangling and hanging on to God and His promises. I didn't want to be vulnerable or feel out of control. I had taught myself through the years to take care of myself so that no one would be able to hurt me too deeply. But I discovered that when I protect myself from people, I shield myself from God too. The internal vows we make ultimately isolate us and cast shadows over the landscape of our lives.

There is something holy that God has tucked into suffering.

This is a key to tapping into the power of allowing Christ, who overcame the world to help you through your troubles and sufferings. You have to finally come to the end of yourself and decide, no matter what the cost, you want to be free to love Christ and follow Him wherever that leads. Even if it means a place where the only thing that keeps you from falling into confusion or despair is grasping His promise to overcome *for you*. I had to decide in the psych ward that I no longer wanted to live a safe, comfortable, cold life. I wanted to live abandoned to God. I began to see that too often I was only willing to give God as much as I could afford to lose or had lost already. But we were not designed to live careful lives, holding back who we really are, our hopes and fears. True strength invites us to live with an open heart and soul, knowing that Christ has a good, strong hold on us.

True strength invites us to live with an open heart and soul, knowing that Christ has a good, strong hold on us.

For me, this meant resigning myself from my self-imposed position as savior and embracing becoming a lamb following her Shepherd.

So when I feel myself pulling away from my closest friends, I choose to reach out and ask them to pray for me rather than retreating into a dark place.

Or when I am aware of someone walking through the nightmare of a child with cancer, I pull in close to her to reinforce that she is not alone, because I know that even in this place Christ is present in the sacrament of suffering.

It is one thing to say, "The LORD is my shepherd, I shall not be in want." It is quite another when you find yourself in a dark place and discover that you are not alone—when you truly begin to rely on God's promise tucked into Psalm 23:4: "Even though I walk through the valley of the shadow of death, I will fear no evil, for you are with me; your rod and your staff, they comfort me."

My diving off the cliff or falling off the edge looked like this: I had gone from one day being the cohost of a nationally syndicated talk show to being in a psychiatric ward of a hospital by that evening. Quite a reversal of fortunes. I thought about Joni that first night. She didn't choose the life she now had. She dove off a platform and broke her neck. I am not for one moment beginning to compare the suffering that Joni continues to experience with anything I have known. But I knew enough of the struggles she faced to know how tempting it is to simply want to opt out of the days and weeks ahead.

Climbing back out of a hole that deep is hard, and there are many painful truths to face as you make the climb. If you have never suffered from serious depression, I think it's hard to understand the physical and mental pain involved. Much of depression is silent and isolating and . . . within. A brain tumor shows up on a CT scan, but depleted brain chemicals do not.

Depression is only one of myriad isolating realities. I think of the woman who has just been told that she cannot have children—the nursery door slams in her face and she will remain an outsider. To the one whose husband looks in her eyes after twenty years of marriage and tells her, "I don't love you anymore. I'm not sure I ever did." Or the woman who looks at herself for the first time in a mirror after the landscape of her femininity has been ravaged by breast cancer. The temptation for those who are looking on is to say, "Pull yourself together. You have so much to be thankful for!" To those who are in the eye of the storm, that is like saying to a child with a crushed leg, "Get up and walk."

The quiet strength I saw in Joni was borne out of the crucible of pain so deep you cannot move, grief so overwhelming it crushes you with the weight of an ocean. But what she found is that when you are pinned, you are held) That didn't prevent her from experiencing the pain or the capacity to hurt, but it gave her an intimacy with Christ that is simply beautiful.

I don't speak of these things lightly. As you read these words, you might be in the middle of unimaginable grief. What I want you to remember or know for the first time is that Christ has been to the bottom of the pit of grief. He tasted the worst dregs that hell can pour out, and He rose again to set us free and secure for us a destiny with Him forever—a destiny that Satan cannot touch. As we walk on our unique path that will take us home, He promises to walk with us and to help us overcome.

By the time Joni and I met again, my life was in a totally different place. I was beginning to understand what Scripture calls the treasures of darkness: "I will give you the treasures of darkness, riches stored in secret places, so that you may know that I am the LORD, the God of Israel, who summons you by name" (Isaiah 45:3). Joni saw that. She told me that when she met me, the first word that came to her mind was *strong*. After my hospitalization, she said, "A different and even better word came to mind: 'gentle,' more so, 'broken and gentle.'"

No matter what circumstances pull the carpet out from underneath us, I found, like millions before me who have walked this path of faith, that God will use the darkest of nights to let us know that He is there, that He upholds us. Christ's words that we have known for years suddenly take on such life and breathe hope. Jesus told those closest to Him, *You are going to have trouble in this world, that is a given. Don't be surprised by it or look anymore for a trouble-free life. Take heart! Strengthen yourself with this absolute truth: I have overcome the world. We win, it's a sure thing. So when you can't hold on any longer, know this—I am holding you. When your strength runs out, I've still got you in My grip, and I'll give you My strength to hold on.*

That is quite a promise. And Jesus' disciples were about to find out just what it meant.

A REVOLUTION FOR THE WEAK

The fact is not lost on me that when Jesus makes His promise to overcome the world (John 16:33), His disciples are thinking things just might be looking up for them and their people. They have been with Jesus for almost three and a half years of ministry. They sense a change and revolution in the air. People follow Jesus and He performs miracles. His teaching is full of authority, but His stories always upend what the people think they know. This is disturbing, especially to the traditionalists among them, and Jesus' life has been threatened by religious officials and rabbis.

Now Jesus has just entered Jerusalem, and the people are greeting Him with praises and spreading their coats on the ground for Him to cross upon (Matthew 21:8–9). The whole city is stirred. The disciples are pointing out the temple buildings to Jesus (Matthew 24:1–2), thinking, *This is it. This is the beginning of Christ coming to us as a new King with a new order.* They don't understand that Jesus has not come to establish an earthly kingdom, even when He tells them that they will be persecuted and suffer for Him (Matthew 24:9).

They don't see that Jesus' life as a man is just hours away from crashing down around Him.

What they do see perplexes them. After raising Lazarus from the dead (John 12:9–10), Jesus does not make a public appearance again. He knows that His time is very short, and for a moment He pulls away from His enemies to be with His closest friends and prepare them for what lies ahead.

So that is the stage set for Jesus' final night with His friends. They go to the Upper Room and prepare to have supper. But first Jesus needs to give them one final lesson, try to show them one more way that He has come to bring revolution and that it must begin in their hearts, not with mustering more of their own strength for the battle but relying solely upon His.

So He grabs a towel, then a water basin, and He begins to wash His disciples' feet.

The disciples are stunned. Their would-be king has just taken on the most demeaning, menial job reserved for non-Jewish slaves. The powerful has chosen the place of the lowliest. Their strong arm has chosen to become weak.

We know that this is how Jesus chose to spend His final hours on earth, in a place of weakness and humility, a place of suffering and not seeming to overcome but to be downtrodden. Had the disciples understood just how little sand there was left to run through the hourglass, they might have asked, *This is overcoming the world*?

Maybe you're asking that even now.

It's a good question, and Jesus' answer is revolutionary: Yes, in weakness there is strength because by taking on our suffering, we can become strong. Jesus' plan, from the very beginning, was to overcome the world not with force, but with love, a violent love stronger than death and that waters cannot quench or rivers overflow (Song of Solomon 8:6–7).

Jesus' plan, from the very beginning, was to overcome the world not with force, but with love.

John's gospel states this at the beginning of the foot-washing scene: "Having loved his own who were in the world, he now showed them the full extent of his love" (John 13:1). In washing His dear friends' feet, Jesus is giving them and us a taste of what He is about to do for all of us—to wash us clean and to use not only water but His very blood. God started giving us clues from the garden of Eden when He killed an animal to make clothes to cover Adam and Eve (Genesis 3:21). And again through the Exodus and desert wanderings when He told the children of Israel to put the blood of a year-old flawless lamb over their doorposts so that the Angel of Death would pass by (Exodus 12:3–13). Then He stopped Abraham's hand as he was about to plunge a dagger into his son Isaac's heart and provided a substitute: a ram caught in the thicket (Genesis 22:9–14). And all the way from Genesis to Revelation—since we are unable to cover ourselves, Christ covers us by the washing of His blood.

Paul writes beautifully to this redefining of strength in his great Christological hymn found in chapter 2 of his letter to the church in Philippi. I highly recommend committing these words to heart. They are severely beautiful as they describe all that Christ left behind:

> [Jesus] made himself nothing,
>> taking the very nature of a servant,
>> being made in human likeness.
> And being found in appearance as a man,
>> he humbled himself
>> and became obedient to death—
>> even death on a cross!
> Therefore God exalted him to the highest place
>> and gave him the name that is above every name,
> that at the name of Jesus every knee should bow,
>> in heaven and on earth and under the earth,
> and every tongue confess that Jesus Christ is Lord,
>> to the glory of God the Father. (Philippians 2:7–11)

Here, the One who spoke everything into being chose to bend His knee and allow the weight and sin of the world to crush Him so that we could be free and His Father would be glorified. The disciples, of course, do not understand this in the Upper Room as Jesus is washing and wiping their feet. And that is when Jesus shows them—and us—one of the most remarkable things about His promise to help us overcome the world, and exactly how He's going to keep that promise.

HIS PRAYERS KEEP THE PROMISE

First, Jesus tells His disciples some disturbing things:

- *To Peter, he will betray Jesus.*
- *To the whole table, just as the world hates Him, it will hate them too.*
- *That they all will be thrown out of the synagogue; and in fact a time is coming when those who put Christ's followers to death will believe that they are doing it for God (John 16:1–2).*
- *And that on this very night, when He needs them the most, they will scatter to their homes and abandon Him.*

Does that sound like the way to strengthen the faint of heart or empower the weak? *What is Jesus doing?*

I believe He is saying, *All of this will happen, but God is still in control.* He is telling Peter, *When you hear yourself doing the very thing you swore you would never do, I understand and I love you.* He is telling His disciples then and us now, *When your world falls apart and nothing makes sense anymore, you are still being held. Nothing that happens will be a surprise to God.* We live on a fallen, broken planet, but Christ has secured our passage all the way home. Or as 2 Corinthians 1:5 puts it: "For just as

144

the sufferings of Christ flow over into our lives, so also through Christ our comfort overflows."

I hear this verse as a gigantic *"Don't panic!"* from our Father.

So with these words, Jesus leads His closest disciples to the Mount of Olives. Luke 22:39 tells us it was common for Jesus to spend time in the garden with God, to withdraw from the world in order to pray. But one thing He does this evening is unusual: He withdraws from the disciples about a stone's throw away. Jesus, our Shelter, our hiding place, is showing that even when we think He is not near, He is within reaching distance. He is with us and ready and, as John 18:4 says, knowing of all the things that are to come upon Him—and us.

And while the disciples sleep, exhausted and spent, Jesus prays. "Father, if you are willing, take this cup from me; yet not my will, but yours be done" (Luke 22:42). Here Christ brings our humanity and the call to servanthood together. Knowing the trouble that lay ahead of Him that night, Christ asks if it is possible to have it removed and yet in the same breath bows His knee to God's will. Our God is not a cosmic eject button, a complete separation from the trials or hardships of this world. If you think about it, how could that mind-set be a demonstration of true strength? Have you ever avoided the hard situation? Shrunk from the confrontation, or bypassed a dream because of the fear of failure? The strength of God is a strength that leans in. And in upholding us with that strength, He empowers us to lean in too.

Before they left the Upper Room that night, Jesus prayed for His friends: "My prayer is not that you take them out of the world but that you protect them from the evil one" (John 17:15). God will protect us, as the verse says. How remarkable, and how giving. In His own moment of uncertainty and grief, profound sadness and fatigue, Jesus asks His Father not to remove us from the world and its troubles, but to protect us. And in the protecting is His request for us to be given strength and endurance and resilience.

Jesus knew what was coming for Him, and He stopped to pray for His disciples, for you, and for me. What a powerful example. His very actions show us that we can face suffering best by not giving into it or pulling into ourselves, but by reaching out and looking up and holding on to this promise. Trouble is knit into the very fabric of this life, but Christ has overcome. The call to take heart implies action, a consciousness. To me this verse says, "Stop! Remember that Christ prepared us for the fact that trouble will come, so gather up everything we are feeling and tuck ourselves into His shelter, the Cleft of the Rock, for He has overcome."

The one thing we all know for sure is that to one degree or another in this world, each of us will suffer. Some people have to bear far more than others. Some may appear to glide through life pain free, but no one escapes unscathed. No matter how hard the circumstances, Jesus assures the faint of heart that He overcame the world and He will help us do the same—and the timing of that promise is important. Just hours before Jesus is to be betrayed by His friends, mocked and beaten, flogged and tortured, nailed to a cross and spit upon—murdered—His heart-to-heart message with His closest friends is this: *Take heart, I have overcome the world.*

And that is the point of the promises. There is a strange but encouraging reality involved in promises and sorrow and the fact that is God is present in the moments of deepest grief, and His arms are wide and clasping. They are strong enough to keep us and strong enough to lift us from this world.

Most of Christ's promises are deeply comforting to me, but there is something in this one promise that I hear in my soul as a battle cry. As I look at the trail that Christ blazed for you and me so that we could be free to love Him and live with Him forever, I want, even in the midst of trouble, to stand! No matter how alone we may feel at moments, because of what Jesus has done for us, we are never alone.

Even in the eye of a storm, we call our hearts to remember that no matter how hard life gets, we win!

❧

No matter how alone we may feel at moments, because of what Jesus has done for us, we are never alone.

Marie & Russell (opp. 29th Russell)

Judy - sister chemo - salvation
    worker worried about
        Kids - Melissa.

Billies - daughter sinus infection

Amber & Wil - move a lot going on.

Marcela Palmar - stint

Sallys friend - Cancer 2 wks to live
        has daughter high School

Jurilyn ?

9

MORE

I Know There's Something Better

THE PROMISE

Ask and it will be given to you; seek and you will find;
knock and the door will be opened to you. For everyone who
asks receives; he who seeks finds; and to him who knocks,
the door will be opened.

—MATTHEW 7:7–8

I can still see their faces and the big cheesy grins that swept from ear
to ear. Christian and his friend Chase sat up in their twin beds like
little princes with room service menus in hand.

I had brought Christian and his buddy with me to Fort Lauderdale,
where I was speaking at a conference that weekend, and had built in
some beach time with the boys. As they had reached the grand old age
of ten, they had requested a room of their own. After choking down a

large laugh, I told them that we would get adjoining rooms, and they would have to leave the door open. After getting them settled, I asked if they wanted to have dinner in their room or in the restaurant. They agreed that room service sounded better. I gave them menus to look at and went to unpack my suitcase.

After a few moments Christian popped his head round the door. "Can I order for Chase and me?" he asked. "I know what to do! Please?"

Christian had been traveling with me since he was six weeks old. I was fairly confident he could handle the task.

"Okay, but if they ask to speak to an adult, I'm right here," I said.

"Okay!" he cried as he dashed back into the next room.

I could hear the boys chatting away and couldn't resist listening.

"So you've done this before?" Chase asked.

"Hundreds of times," Christian replied.

"And we don't need money?" Chase prodded.

"No, dude, it's like a miracle," Christian answered. "You just call up and order whatever you want, and they bring it up on a tray and you just sign a piece of paper and that's it."

"Wow!" Chase said.

"I know, right? Wow!" Christian echoed.

I waited until I heard the knock on their door and stood in the entranceway that connected our rooms to make sure that whoever was delivering their food saw that they were not alone. Christian dutifully signed the check, and I showed the server out. When I turned around, I saw for the first time what they had actually ordered: two large pepperoni pizzas—one for each of them—a pint of ice cream, and a pot of hot chocolate.

"Look at all this, Mom," Christian announced triumphantly. "And it didn't cost us a thing!"

I tried not to laugh, but it was a struggle! That night I explained the inner workings of room service to my son and his mesmerized friend. I told them that, yes, there are wonderful things for the asking—and, no, you do not receive if you do not ask—but there really is no such thing as a free lunch. Christian sighed and asked, "Oh Mom, is this another one of those teaching moments?"

As I reflected on that evening, it both horrified and amused me to think that they could have just gone down the whole menu and ordered everything on there! Instead, they went for good ol' boy food. Granted, it wasn't the most nutritious meal, and they both looked distinctly uncomfortable afterward as they lay on top of their beds like beached whales, but boy did we have a good laugh.

I began to think about their order and wondered if, in many ways, we do something similar in our relationship with God. Our heavenly Father offers us so much more than a room-service menu, and His resources are unlimited! But like Christian and his friend, we settle for ordering junk food when that seems appealing while God offers us a bountiful gourmet meal of His presence in every moment of our lives.

A PROMISE FOR MORE

Too often we settle for small, temporal things in place of the great, spiritual wealth God wants to give us. No wonder, that right at the end of His first recorded sermon, the Sermon on the Mount, Jesus gives this promise, "Ask and it will be given to you; seek and you will find; knock and the door will be opened to you. For everyone who asks receives; he who seeks finds; and to him who knocks, the door will be opened." (Matthew 7:7–8).

On first read you might be tempted to think this promise plays into our more self-indulgent side, but when you dig deep, there is unmined treasure underneath the first pass. What Jesus is promising is a radical transformation in how we think and how we live. I can see the people leaning in when Jesus tells them this on that hillside. When He sat down to teach (an indication to the crowd that He was adopting the position of a teaching rabbi), the people drew closer. But what they were about to hear would shock them as much as if Jesus had suddenly yelled in their faces—because His promise to us, like that sermon, is about *more*. Whatever we ask, He has more in store. What He is about to say will change everything if we understand the promise.

> *What Jesus is promising is a radical transformation*
> *in how we think and how we live.*

Matt 6:45

Certainly the people on that hillside didn't expect what Jesus was going to say that day. He was teaching with authority; they got that. But His words and this promise would blow them away. He would give them comfort and then issue a challenge. He would tell them it was the heart that mattered, and then say that because of the heart, we should live higher, with more abandon and passion. He would tell the people that God is not distant or disapproving or disconnected, but a Father who loves to give good gifts to His children. So they should ask and ask and keep on asking.

Lean In and Listen

To understand how striking Jesus' promise is, you have to picture the scene and put yourself in the place of the people who first heard it. The Sermon on the Mount was no simple sermon of niceties. Rather, it was like U2 at Red Rocks Amphitheatre. There was shock and there was awe. Jesus didn't ease into the teaching that day or begin with a lovely greeting to the people. He blew them away.

A friend of mine who is a speaking coach explains it this way: when you address a crowd, the first sentence out of your mouth is crucial as it can either resonate with your audience and grab attention, arresting your listeners, or fall flat and cause people to tune out.

Well, the first word out of Christ's mouth riveted the crowd because it's not a word ever associated with them: *blessed*. The word in the Greek is *makarios*, which means "happy" when applied to men or women, but when applied to God means "the glory of the gospel." In Paul's first letter to Timothy, he uses that word as he writes of "the glorious gospel of the blessed God" (1 Timothy 1:11).

This is notable because the word *blessed* was a powerful word to those who heard Jesus that day. To them it meant "divine joy, perfect happiness" and described the kind of joy believed only to be experienced by the gods or the dead. It was used in pagan Greek literature of the day to describe happiness that only they could know.[1] *Blessed* implied an inner security and rest that didn't depend on outward circumstances or an ability to keep the rules for happiness. This was so much more than the Jews could have hoped for. They strived to be acceptable, to escape judgment, but to be blessed—what a gift.

So you can see why this was a revolutionary concept to Jesus' audience. The Pharisees, their intellectual and zealous gatekeepers, had taught them that righteousness was tied to external behavior, a matter of obeying rules and regulations of which there were many. The Pharisees had taught that praying, giving, fasting, and keeping all the other dietary and Sabbath rules could measure one's righteousness.

But in the Beatitudes, Jesus described how character flowed from inside the human heart. This was not a list of things to tick off as tasks completed at the end of the day but rather a radical new way to live, sold out to God. Jesus wasn't selling memberships to a club but calling people to join a new kingdom that would cost them everything they had but would give them everything they needed. Can you imagine if you have spent your whole life trying to keep every little nitpicky rule to try to find favor with God and suddenly you hear that what really matters is your heart?

Now, when I say nitpicky rules, I mean nitpicky rules. Here are just a few examples.

- *On the Sabbath (shabbat in Hebrew, related to the verb shavat, meaning "to cease, desist, to rest"), if you put out a lamp because someone in the house was sick and you wanted him to be able to sleep, that was not breaking the law. But if you put out the lamp just to save oil, that was breaking the law.*
- *If a Jewish sailor was caught in a storm after sunset on Friday and touched the helm, even simply to save his life or the lives of his passengers, that was breaking the law.*
- *Treatment to alleviate toothache pain in those days was to put vinegar on the offending tooth, but if you did that on the Sabbath, you were breaking the law. If, however, you put a lot of vinegar on your food that day and it had the side effect of stopping the toothache, the rabbis would say, "If he is healed, he is healed."*

Crazy, don't you think?

JESUS RAISES THE BAR

Do you see how complicated and stressful life, with these laws, was for the Jewish people? What a relief then when Jesus spoke, and the first word out of His mouth was "blessed"—and even more astonishing when He listed specific people who are blessed: the poor in spirit, those who mourn, the meek, those who hunger and thirst for righteousness, the merciful, the pure in heart, the peacemakers, those who are persecuted for righteousness' sake, and those reviled or persecuted on account of Christ (Matthew 5:1–12).

I can imagine the crowd being initially stunned but then heartened by Jesus' promise of a blessed life. These listeners were a persecuted people, after all. The Romans ruled over their lives and taxed them into poverty. The Romans even used Jewish people to extract ridiculous taxes and turned a blind eye to those who took more than was required and pocketed the rest. I'm sure there was no more despised group of people than the Jews who worked for the Romans and used the power of the Roman boot to line their own pockets.

One of these men was Zacchaeus. His name means "pure," but his life belied his name—he'd become rich at the expense of those around him. But Zacchaeus discovered that there is something intrinsically disappointing built into everything this world offers, and what he really needed only Jesus could give him. Zacchaeus had connived his way into great wealth, but his spiritual poverty was wretched. He was starving to death for what mattered, for what would last. In a dramatic encounter with Christ, Zacchaeus received more than he had ever dared to ask or dream. We'll look at his story in a moment.

Not only had the Romans oppressed the Jewish people, but the leaders sent by God to guide and love His people had worn them into the ground with petty rules and regulations. There was no joy or grace or freedom, just a merciless yardstick that told the story of how far short they fell every single day. And here was a man who not only spoke out against their oppression but drove the issue deeper, into their hearts and the oppression that waged within.

Then Jesus' message got more complicated. He told the crowd that they are salt and light. If salt loses its flavor, He said, it's no use anymore. And it's the same with a light—if you hide a lamp under a basket, it doesn't help anyone at all. Then Jesus dropped a bombshell:

Do not think that I have come to abolish the Law or the Prophets; I have not come to abolish them but to fulfill them. I tell you the truth, until heaven and earth disappear, not the smallest letter, not the least stroke of a pen, will by any means disappear from the Law until everything is accomplished. Anyone who breaks one of the least of these commandments and teaches others to do the same will be called least in the kingdom of heaven, but whoever practices and teaches these commands will be called great in the kingdom of heaven. For I tell you that unless your righteousness surpasses that of the Pharisees and the teachers of the law, you will certainly not enter the kingdom of heaven. (Matthew 5:17–20)

So not only did observance of the Law matter, but you couldn't change the interpretation by a tiny stroke. You had to be exact.

Can you imagine the people thinking, *Okay, Lord, You had me for a bit there, but now You've lost me completely! First of all, You tell me that what matters is my heart, but then You tell me that unless my righteousness exceeds those who have been holding these laws over our lives, I'm not getting into heaven? That gives me no hope at all.*

Live Higher, Lean Harder

Having initially brought much-needed comfort and hope to the crowd on the hill that day, Jesus then presented the people with an impossible task: to keep the letter of the law even more than the most devout Jewish leader. It was as if He delivered to the people the most wonderful room service, servings of just what they needed, with greater richness than they even imagined, and then reminded them there is a high price to pay.

How can we do that? the people must have thought when Jesus said to keep the law even beyond the letter, to the heart. How can we live this impossible demand?

Their religious leaders were supposed to be present in their lives and bring them comfort and hope. Instead, the Pharisees had done nothing but add to the harshness of life for the people. And now this Jesus, who had spoken so comfortingly to them, with such refreshment for their spirits, was talking about not only living out the letter of the law, but way beyond it.

The people must have been spent.

And that's when Jesus did the most remarkable thing yet. He looked at the crowd, and I can only imagine the love contained in His eyes, and said, "Do not worry about your life." He promised that the Father cares for us and waits for us to come to Him when we are lost, when we need direction, or when we are longing for answers.

So after this long and at times confusing sermon comes this outrageous promise that invites us not to expect less but rather to ask for much more from a Father who loves us and knows our real needs: "Ask, and it will be given to you; seek and you will find; knock and the door will be opened to you. For everyone who asks receives; he who seeks finds; and to him who knocks, the door will be opened" (Matthew 7:7).

For "ask," Jesus used the word *aiteo*, meaning "to entreat, to beg, or to supplicate." The word implied a distinction in position and circumstances between the parties, and expressed a petition from an inferior to a superior. (A distinction, it's worth noting, that Christ never used when He talked to the Father.)

For "seek," He used the word *zeteo*, meaning "to seek after, look for, strive to find."

For "knock," He used the word *krouo*, meaning "to knock at the door with a heavy blow."

Jesus was saying: *Shout to God. Run to Him. Chase Him down. Bang on His door anytime, day or night. Live higher, with all your heart, but lean harder on God, with all that's in you—and you will find God there, always ready, ever waiting to give you even beyond what you need.*

157

*Live higher, with all your heart, but lean harder on God,
with all that's in you—and you will find God there, always
ready, ever waiting to give you even beyond what you need.*

Are Our Desires Too Weak?

This is an incredible message! Jesus not only reminds us that God waits to give to us what we seek and has an ever-open door for the asking, but that He will deliver beyond what we even know we want or need.

I love the way C. S. Lewis put it in *The Weight of Glory*:

If there lurks in most modern minds the notion that to desire our own good and earnestly to hope for the enjoyment of it is a bad thing, I submit that this notion has crept in from Kant and the Stoics and is no part of the Christian faith. Indeed, if we consider the unblushing promises of reward and the staggering nature of the rewards promised in the Gospels, it would seem that our Lord finds our desires, not too strong, but too weak. We are half-hearted creatures, fooling about with drink and sex and ambition when infinite joy is offered us, like an ignorant child who wants to go on making mud pies in a slum because he cannot imagine what is meant by the offer of a holiday at the sea. We are far too easily pleased.[2]

Ask, Seek, Knock for What?

At the end of the Sermon on the Mount comes an invitation that Christ ties in directly to what every father in the crowd would understand—the most primal desire to provide for your children:

> Ask and it will be given to you; seek and you will find; knock and
> the door will be opened to you. For everyone who asks receives; he
> who seeks finds; and to him who knocks, the door will be opened.
>
> Which of you, if his son asks for bread, will give him a stone?
> Or if he asks for a fish, will give him a snake? If you, then, though
> you are evil, know how to give good gifts to your children, how
> much more will your Father in heaven give good gifts to those who
> ask him! (Matthew 7:7–11)

Many commentators see these verses standing alone as a separate piece. It's what's called a *pericope*. No, I did not just misspell *periscope*! The prefix *peri* is from the Greek. It means "about," "around," or "beyond." The rest of the word, *cope*, is from the Greek *kope*, which means "a cutting." It is pronounced "ko-pay." A *pe-ri-ko-pay* is a section of text from a book or a document. It has been "cut around" and identified as a literary unit.[3] The important thing about each pericope or section is that it be studied as a whole. So if we look at these five verses, we see Christ acknowledging that we have great needs in life and there is only one way to have those needs met. The answer is clear: prayer, prayer, prayer. And not just a faint, halfhearted request but an intentional, committed, relentless pursuit of God.

Ask and it will be *given* to you—not lent or sold to you, but *given*.

Seek and you *will* find—not that you might find or I hope you find, but you *will* find.

Knock and the door *will* be opened to you—not that it might be opened or only opened if someone's home, but it *will* be opened to you.

Then it might be reasonable for someone who is in the listening crowd to ask, "How do we know that's true? What are you basing this on?" This is where the analogy of our relationship with our heavenly Father and the relationship between a father and son comes in, and it is powerful. The examples Jesus chooses at first might not say much to us, but to His audience, they would have great significance. Matthew gives us two and when Luke relates the story he adds in another (Luke 11:12).

In Matthew we read, "Which of you, if his son asks for bread, will give him a stone? Or if he asks for a fish, will give him a snake?" Luke adds, "Or if he asks for an egg, will give him a scorpion?" These are unlikely pairings to us, but Jesus' audience would have a clear picture of what that would look like. The small, round limestone rocks on the seashore would look exactly like the small loaves of bread a mother would put in her son's lunchbox. So Jesus asks, "What father would trick his son and, instead of giving him the bread he needs, swap it out for a stone?"

The next question is, what father would give his boy a serpent if he asked for a fish? The serpent alluded to would probably be an eel, which according to Jewish dietary laws was unclean (Leviticus 11:12). Christ is saying, *What dad, when his son asks him for a fish, would mock him by giving him a fish but one he couldn't eat? How cruel would that be?*

Next up, the scorpion and the egg. When a scorpion is folded up and at rest, the pale ones look exactly like an egg but in reality would be terrifying to a child. The scorpion's sting is very painful and can even be deadly. Jesus asks, *What father would look into the eyes of a hungry child and give him something that would scare and harm him?*

Jesus is saying that if those of us who are part of this fallen, broken world wouldn't do that but rather run to answer our child's needs, how much more will God, who knows us and loves us, run to meet our needs? But not only that. God's love for us is so far above what we think we need, and His answers spring out of the depth of His mercy and wisdom.

THE GIFT OF ASKING ONE
WHO KNOWS AND LOVES US

Do you ever find yourself asking, "God, why didn't You answer that prayer? I needed to hear from You today on that. Don't You hear me? Don't You love me?"

In his commentary on Matthew's gospel, William Barclay tells of the Greeks and their gods and how they answered prayers. He tells the story of Aurora, goddess of the dawn, who falls in love with a mortal, named Tithonus. When Aurora realizes that one day Tithonus will die and she will not, she asks Zeus, king of the gods, for one gift for this young man. He agrees to answer one request, so she asks that Tithonus will live forever. What she did not think to do was ask that he would remain forever young, so he grows older and older and older and cannot die. The gift becomes a curse.

In contrast, as Barclay writes, "God will always answer our prayers: *but He will answer them in His way*, and His way will be the way of perfect wisdom and perfect love."[4]

Not Once, Not Twice, but Over and Over

In Greek language structure, there are two types of imperatives or commands. One is the *aorist*, which is a onetime command such as, "Take the dogs for a walk." Then there is the *present imperative*, which would be an ongoing command, like "You are the one who always takes the dogs for a walk." When we read *ask, seek, knock* in Matthew 7:7–8, all three words are written in the present imperative, which means never stop asking, never stop seeking, never stop knocking.

This promise is beautiful and powerful and calls us to action. God is the one who fully knows us and loves us, so we come to our Father as children who are dearly loved and ask, ask, and keep on asking!

God, out of the depth of His grace and love, gives us so much more than we would even know to ask for.

Just ask Zacchaeus.

FROM AN OUTCAST TO A PLACE OF HONOR

We read the story of Zacchaeus in Luke 19:1–10:

> Jesus entered Jericho and was passing through. A man was there by the name of Zacchaeus; he was a chief tax collector and was wealthy. He wanted to see who Jesus was, but being a short man he could not, because of the crowd. So he ran ahead and climbed a sycamore-fig tree to see him, since Jesus was coming that way.
>
> When Jesus reached the spot, he looked up and said to him, "Zacchaeus, come down immediately. I must stay at your house today." So he came down at once and welcomed him gladly. All the people saw this and began to mutter, "He has gone to be the guest of a 'sinner.'" But Zacchaeus stood up and said to the Lord, "Look, Lord! Here and now I give half of my possessions to the poor, and if I have cheated anybody out of anything, I will pay back four times the amount." Jesus said to him, "Today salvation has come to this house, because this man, too, is a son of Abraham. For the Son of Man came to seek and to save what was lost."

Zacchaeus was a "chief tax collector," which means he held a higher rank in the Roman tax collection system than Matthew did when Jesus called him to be a disciple. It's clear that he had become a very wealthy man in that region. Jericho was a significant center of commerce, stationed along a major trade route connecting Jerusalem and its surrounding areas with the lands east of the Jordan. We are not told anything about Zacchaeus's personal life, whether he was married or had children, but one thing is clear—he was not a happy man. He had everything that so often we are told will make us happy, but it was not enough.

I think that must be one of the most disillusioning places to be in life. We live in a culture that tells us various lies:

If you were thinner, you'd be happier.
If you were married to someone else, you'd be happier.
If you had more money, you'd be happier.

The list goes on and on.

So what happens if you are one of the "rich and famous" and you have all the things that you are told will make you happy, and they just don't? I think that was the life that Zacchaeus led until one day he heard that this man Jesus was coming through Jericho.

Zacchaeus was determined to find out what all the fuss was about. He took off and, I would imagine without even realizing it, became one who was asking and seeking and knocking. He ran ahead of the crowd and climbed up into a tree, knowing that his slight stature would make it hard for him to see over the crowd. What he could never have known was that God was looking for him too.

When Jesus looked up into the tree and addressed Zacchaeus by name, I bet he almost fell out! Then Jesus did something that no other Jew would have done: He came to Zacchaeus's home. It doesn't get more personal than that. That one encounter changed his life for eternity. I wonder how long Zacchaeus had been waiting for someone to see beyond his terrible choices that had left him isolated and alone with his cold piles of money all around him?

So Much More

Zacchaeus's life was changed. He gave half of what he had to the poor, and if he had cheated anyone, he gave it back to them fourfold. Church history tells us that Zacchaeus went on to become the bishop of Caesarea. He wanted a glimpse of God and became His honored servant. When you pursue God, only He knows what will become of you. Zacchaeus experienced more than he ever thought possible.

As I think back to those two little boys on the edge of their beds marveling over the magic of a room-service menu and how radical it was to order a whole pizza each, I think God looks down at us and says, *My child, don't settle for what will feed you for a moment. Ask for more! There is so much more I want to give you. You long to know My presence and I long to reveal Myself to you if you will ask. You seek happiness in places that only bring disappointment and pain, but if you seek Me, I will be found, and you will be filled. You knock timidly at My door wondering if you have a right to even be there, and I say knock with everything that is in you, and I will throw the doors of heaven open. I know you so well. I know the storms that have washed over you, and I call you to My side. I AM your Shelter.*

Hear Him answer your call:

If you ask, I will answer.
If you seek, you will find.
If you knock, I will open the door.

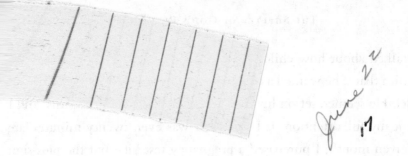

June 2 '17 (handwritten)

10

HOME *Hope*

I Have a Future

THE PROMISE

In my Father's house are many rooms; if it were not so, I would have told you. I am going there to prepare a place for you.

—JOHN 14:2

I will never forget the moment when I discovered that I was pregnant. I was shocked and overwhelmed with emotions. I was not one of those girls who had always longed for motherhood. I loved other people's babies, but the thought of taking care of such a fragile human being was daunting to me. I thought of myself as more of a cat-and-dog mother.

At thirty-nine, I had made peace with the reality that most likely I would never be the mother of a child by natural means. Barry and I had married later in life. I was thirty-seven and he was thirty-two. We had talked about how children might not be possible with me, and I told him that if he wanted a quiverful, he might have to find a younger model. He seemed set on his choice. We tried for a few months, and I gave it my full attention. If I felt that I was even twenty minutes late any given month, I purchased a pregnancy test kit—but the plus sign never appeared. I decided that I didn't want to get entrenched in that monthly ritual of hoping and disappointment, so I set the issue on the back shelf of my mind.

In March 1996, Barry and I were in Florida for a few days. I was performing a concert at Dr. D. James Kennedy's church in Coral Ridge, and we decided to take a break from our normal schedules back in Southern California and just enjoy a change of scenery.

Well, you know the saying: when you stop pursuing something, that's often the time it arrives unannounced. A few weeks later I was aware of being a little more tired than normal, particularly after a mini-vacation. I felt a little queasy when I woke up. Yet I didn't put two and two together. Not until one day, when I was cleaning out my bathroom cabinet and saw that I still had one pregnancy testing kit left over from the jumbo box I had purchased at Costco. I almost threw it in the trash, but on a whim I thought I'd take it anyway. I took the test and put it on the window ledge and forgot all about it. (Dear germophobes, I do apologize!)

Later that afternoon, I saw it and, a little horrified that I'd just left it sitting there, picked it up and threw it in the trash. I remember that moment now as if it happened in slow motion. As the test stick fell into the trash, it spun a couple of times and something caught my eye. It landed result-side down in the bottom of the freshly cleaned-out trash can.

Did I just see a plus sign?

I realize that most of you would have immediately grabbed the thing and turned it over, but I didn't. I sat on the floor beside the can and peered in.

How could such an innocent piece of plastic have
change my world?

My mind flashed back to when my sister, Frances, was in the
Queen Mother's Maternity Hospital in Glasgow, Scotland. Frances,
who is two years older than I, had just given birth to a baby boy, David,
and asked me if I wanted to hold him.

"What if I drop him?" I said.

"You won't drop him," she replied with a smile.

"Remember, Frances, I drop things!"

"Then sit in the chair, and Ian will bring him to you," she said.

My brother-in-law put this tiny little person wrapped up like a
burrito into my arms, and I just stared at him.

"Hello, wee one," I said. "I'm your aunt, but I don't want that to
worry you. I'll practice carrying things around the house like melons
or the cat. I'll get better at this."

He closed his eyes and went to sleep.

I thought of his sweetness as I sat there next to the trash bin.
Having a baby of my own, being pregnant, would change everything
in my world. I picked the stick out of the trash and set it on the floor,
still results-side down.

"Well, Lord, here is what I'm thinking: If this is negative, You just
don't have it in Your plan for me to be a mother, and that's probably a
good thing as I did drop the melon and the cat. If, on the other hand, it
is positive, You are okay with this and You will help me, right? Because
even though You made melons and cats, You can help me to hold on to
a baby for longer than twenty minutes, right?"

With that, I turned over the test stick and there it was: positive!

I cried for a long time.

Then I danced. And then I went into the spare room where we
kept all the Christmas ornaments and wedding gifts that I was not
quite sure what to do with (but didn't want to give away in case Aunt

Maude came to visit) and thought, *This will be your home now, little one. Do you like pink or blue?*

THE PROMISE OF A TRUE HOME

It was one thing for me at thirty-nine with a penchant for dropping things to discover that I was going to have a baby to bring home. But can you even begin to imagine what it must have been like for Mary, mother of Jesus? Her life and world open up one of the most beautiful promises of God to us, the Ultimate Promise, you could say, and that is the promise of eternity with Him, because He is our home.

> *Mary's life and world open up one of the most beautiful promises of God to us, the Ultimate Promise, you could say, and that is the promise of eternity with Him, because He is our home.*

Jesus' promise to us before His execution, "I am going . . . to prepare a place for you" (John 14:2), would have unique significance and power for Mary. The mother of Jesus had not been able to prepare much of a place for this little one the night He was born. Perhaps she wondered if anything she had been able to give Him would be enough.

This is how the birth of Jesus Christ came about: His mother Mary was pledged to be married to Joseph, but before they came together, she was found to be with child through the Holy Spirit. (Matthew 1:18)

Girls in Mary's time were betrothed or engaged when they were twelve or thirteen. It was not an engagement as we know it that could be broken off at any point up until the wedding with no legal ramifications. No, this was a formal bond that could only be broken by a decree of divorce and usually lasted for a year, during which time no sexual activity was to take place. The Old Testament rules for any immorality occurring during the engagement were as follows:

> If a man happens to meet in a town a virgin pledged to be married and he sleeps with her, you shall take both of them to the gate of that town and stone them to death—the girl because she was in a town and did not scream for help, and the man because he violated another man's wife. You must purge the evil from among you. (Deuteronomy 22:23–24)

One obviously did not want to have a soft voice in those days! The rules went on to say that if the offense took place in the countryside, then only the man should be put to death because even if the young girl screamed, no one but the sheep would have heard her. The engagement period was thought to have been a year to make sure that the girl was not pregnant by another man.

Do you see the enormity of what was about to happen to Mary and how those who knew her would view it? This shows us a lot about the kind of girl she was and the kind of man Joseph was, and it helps us consider all that they went through to cling to this promise of the Messiah coming to their home in order to make a way for all of us to find the way back to our one true home, heaven, with Christ, who is our Shelter.

How Could It End Like This?

Since we all know how the story ends, let's start there. Mary may have been slight, but she was strong. Everything within her wanted to fall to the dry ground that was absorbing His blood like a ravenous animal. Rather, she stood and never took her eyes off His face and watched as He struggled to breathe. How she longed to hold Him one more time as she had done when He was just a little boy running home with scraped knees. She wanted to touch His face and wipe the blood that was crusting in His eyes in the merciless heat. She looked at His hands now cruelly nailed to wood and remembered how He had learned the feel of wood and nails from His father, to hold together not to tear apart, to create beauty, not to destroy it.

To one side, the soldiers gambled for the seamless garment she had made for Him. They had considered tearing it into pieces and sharing it and for some reason did not.

"Father, forgive them, for they do not know what they are doing" (Luke 23:34).

His voice was raspy and dry, but she heard every word. Even in this cauldron of pain they had not changed Him. They could nail His wrists to a tree, but they could not nail their bitterness into His heart, no matter what they did to Him. She wondered if they even heard His words. "They do not know what they are doing." It was just six words, but the understatement spoke volumes. As those words perched on her fragile soul, she thought, *If they knew, would there still be forgiveness?* He spoke again. This time He was speaking to just one man, to one of those being executed beside Him.

"I tell you the truth, today you will be with me in paradise" (Luke 23:43).

The criminal being executed beside her son did not begin that day in faith. He had mocked and cried out with the rest of them until he heard those first words: Forgive them . . .

Forgive them! That such a thing was still possible in this broken and

170

barbaric place was stunning, impossible. She watched the man struggle and twist his body to look into her son's eyes, and he saw what she knew.

Behold, the Lamb of God, who takes away the sin of the world.

In these last moments on this earth, this wretched soul found freedom. Mary wondered if the criminal's mother was in the crowd somewhere. He had been a little boy once too. He had sat on his mother's lap and told her everything he was going to do when he grew up. This barbaric end had never been part of that dream. Had this mother watched through the years as their dreams turned into nightmares? Mary hoped that if the mother was there that she witnessed this exchange of death and despair for life and freedom. *hope*

Jesus spoke again, and this time it was to her: "Dear woman, here is your son."

Then to John, his dearest friend: "Here is your mother." (John 19:26–27).

As Jesus turned His full attention on her, He looked deep into her soul. The love in that gaze was almost more painful to bear than watching His battered body struggle for air. He didn't call her "Mother"; He called her "woman." He had called her that before at the wedding in Cana, but she knew this time it was good-bye. How could one woman's heart contain this much pain without tearing apart? For the first time, she was glad that Joseph was no longer here on this earth. To watch his boy battered and bruised would have been more than he could have taken. Only women's hearts are made for such things. She felt the warmth of John's arm wrap around her shoulders. How she loved this young man. She knew why Jesus felt as He did about him, the tender love, care, and devotion. John would take care of her now, and she would let him rest his head and sob on her breast.

Jesus spoke again: "I am thirsty" (John 19:28).

What a bitter irony! She recalled His invitation that had wreaked

171

havoc in the temple that day: "If anyone is thirsty, let him come to me and drink" (John 7:37).

That invitation had split the crowd. Some tried to arrest Him, and some thought He'd come to rescue them, but few if any understood the offer.

She watched as one of the soldiers dipped a sponge into the wine and held it to His lips. The pungent smell of the wine carried on the breeze reached Mary, and in a moment she was back to that day in Cana when everything began. He had called her "woman" that day too. His gaze had penetrated the pondering places in her heart when He asked her, "What does this have to do with me?" He said that day that His hour had not yet come. Mary agonized over the thought that perhaps she hurried her son to this slaughterhouse. He spoke just once more, three words: "It is finished" (John 19:30).

As He bowed His head, Mary knew that He was gone. But the way He bowed his head was so deliberate. It wasn't as one beaten to death in body and spirit, but as one laying His head down after a long, long day with an impossible task completed. It was a quiet declaration of victory.

As Joseph of Arimathea and Nicodemus lowered Christ's body onto a clean, white sheet, did Mary think back to the night when He was born and they wrapped Him tight to keep Him warm?

The Least of These

Mary was a Jewess from the tribe of Judah, and she was engaged to Joseph, who was a carpenter in Nazareth. The Jews in Galilee, and especially those from Nazareth, were looked down on as nonkosher because of the mixed population of Jew and Gentile there. (Remember when Nathaniel said, "Can anything good come out of Nazareth?") It's clear that Mary and Joseph came from poor families. We know that because after Jesus was born, the sacrificial gift brought to the temple was two turtledoves or pigeons, not a lamb (Leviticus 12:8). This was a provision made for the poorest of the poor. God not only chose a young girl from the wrong side of the tracks but from a very humble family. If you ever feel that you don't measure up to those around you who come from well-educated or well-to-do families, remember the kind of family in which God chose to place His Son.

There are many times when I stand onstage in a packed arena, looking out at the faces of thousands of women, and think back to the night of my eighth-grade dance. I was so excited about the evening and wanted the perfect dress. The fashion that year was short, straight dresses, but before I could talk to my mom about it, she told me that she had my dress. A family at church had given it to me, and she told me that it was upstairs on my bed.

I will never forget how long it took me to climb those stairs, praying that for once I would have the right thing to wear. It was hard for my mom to raise three children alone after my father's death, and it meant that I wore hand-me-downs most of the time. I opened the bedroom door, and there lying on the bed was the wrong dress. It was powder blue and frilly and full. I sat on the floor and cried. I knew how much it meant to my mom to have provided me with a dress, and I would not show her my tears of disappointment. So on the night of the dance, I put my dress on, smiling big, and walked the two blocks to school.

As I got close, I could see all my friends arriving with the right dresses on, so I spent the evening in the field beside the school. I couldn't go in, but I couldn't let my mom know, so I stayed till the dance was over and went home. I was the scared child in our family. I was the one who could not travel for more than two miles in a car without throwing up. I am the least likely to be asked to carry the Lamb of God across the nation and stand in front of large crowds, but God chooses to place His life in unlikely arms.

That must have been how Mary felt—but how much more?

The angel went to her and said, "Greetings, you who are highly favored! The Lord is with you." Mary was greatly troubled at his words and wondered what kind of greeting this might be. But the angel said to her, "Do not be afraid, Mary, you have found favor with God. You will be with child and give birth to a son, and you are to give him the name Jesus." (Luke 1:28–31)

There is no account of anyone else being with Mary when the angel greeted her. I think it would have been much easier for her if Gabriel had appeared when she was having dinner with her family. Then she would have had eyewitnesses to this unprecedented event. But that's not what happened. Mary would have to carry this sacred charge alone for some time. (We'll look at God's grace in sending an angel to Joseph as well later.) What is amazing to me is that Mary doesn't question how the pregnancy will impact her life, only how it would be possible as she was still a virgin. God is never grieved by our honest questions, just our unbelief.

God is never grieved by our honest questions, just our unbelief.

You might remember that before the angel visited Mary, he visited Zechariah. The angel said, "Do not be afraid, Zechariah; your prayer has been heard. Your wife Elizabeth will bear you a son, and you are to give him the name John" (Luke 1:13). Zechariah didn't believe that could happen and was struck dumb until John was born. But Mary believed she could bear the Son of God—she just wanted to know how God would make it happen.

When she is told that she will conceive by the Holy Spirit, she utters these words, "I am the Lord's servant. May it be to me as you have said" (Luke 1:38).

Here we have a poor, young teenager welcoming the will of God, knowing what it will cost her. She will have to tell her parents and her fiancé, knowing that by law Joseph can publicly disgrace her, and she will never be able then to find a husband. She could even be stoned to death. Mary first tells Joseph, who is obviously devastated but doesn't want to hurt Mary more than he has to, so he decides to divorce her quietly. God, in His mercy, sends an angel to Joseph to let him know that Mary is speaking the truth. In his greeting, the angel reminds Joseph of his own royal lineage as a son of David: "An angel of the Lord appeared to him in a dream and said, 'Joseph son of David, do not be afraid to take Mary home as your wife, because what is conceived in her is from the Holy Spirit. She will give birth to a son, and you are to give him the name Jesus, because he will save his people from their sins'" (Matthew 1:20–21).

Through a Mother's Eyes

What must Mary have thought as she watched Jesus grow into a man? How many things might she have wondered about Him as she saw Him perform miracles and wonders at the beginning of His ministry? (This tiny one they welcomed into their humble home had grown into a man who was redefining what home is, who family is, what our future can look like.)

That first miracle, for instance, at a friend's wedding, Mary saw Jesus take something ordinary and make it exceptional. There is no mention of Joseph in accounts of this event. Most commentators agree that Joseph had died and Mary was alone at the wedding with Jesus and the five disciples whom Jesus had called at that point. The parents, who were most likely friends of Mary's, had run out of wine. Wedding feasts in that culture lasted for seven days, and it was a terrible thing

to run out of food or wine. The parents could actually be fined if supplies ran out. So Mary made Jesus aware of the issue and watched to
see what He might do.

Christ's response seemed harsh. Translators have softened the
Greek a little to read as, "Dear woman, why do you involve me?"
The literal translation of John 2:4 is, "Woman, what to me, and to
you?" Christ made it clear to Mary that day that He was now strictly
on His Father's schedule. Did she ever think, *But that's not how we do
things in our home?*

Mary told the servers to do whatever Jesus said, and then she said
no more. As she watched that day, she knew it had begun. Wine at a
wedding was a small thing, but it had begun. Then came the miracles
of healing and of feeding massive crowds, as His popularity grew. But
she knew there was a change in the wind, a tide turning, as the Jewish
religious leaders began to take a stand against Christ. When He was
a little boy, she could use the four walls of her home to protect Him,
but no more.

Did God see what was happening?

Did It All Go Wrong?

As Mary watched Jesus in agony on the cross, it must have seemed
as if that tide turned so quickly. Did Mary understand that this was
part of the plan, or did she believe that darkness had put out the light?
Jesus' words to the thief on the cross offered him a life beyond this
life. But when, where? I wonder if Mary thought back to her response
to Gabriel that day: "I am the Lord's servant," she had answered.
"May it be to me as you have said" (Luke 1:38).

May it be it to me as You have said.

What large words. What a big idea. Did Mary want to take them
back? Don't you think she must have questioned God's plan and if
He was even in control? Haven't we all been there at times? Would

176

any mother be able to say this as she watched her son tortured and murdered?

Standing at the foot of the cross, as a sign was roughly nailed above Jesus' head—JESUS OF NAZARETH, KING OF THE JEWS—Mary must have thought back to the gifts brought by those noble men from the East. There had been gold and frankincense—gifts fit for a king. The third gift, the myrrh, now made sense. Myrrh was an herb used to embalm the dead. As Mary watched her son's lifeless, bloodied body, did she wonder, *Is this it? Is it all over now? What did I not understand?*

The Pain of Disappointment

I saved this promise, "I have gone to prepare a place for you," until the last chapter for a couple of reasons. There are some things in this life that have no answer this side of eternity. Even some of Christ's promises don't always make sense in the light of what we are experiencing. Many moments in life feel unredeemed. Ask any parent who has buried a child, or one who has watched a loved one suffer greatly and die. Ask if it seems to them that good has come out of it.

Now, I am not for a second saying that God's promises are not 100 percent trustworthy—they are the unassailable shelter of His goodness. What I am saying is that some questions might only be answered when we get home. Some wounds are hard to heal this side of eternity.

Some questions might only be answered when we get home. Some wounds are hard to heal this side of eternity.

I think of Todd and Angie Smith and the story Angie shares in her book *I Will Carry You.* You may know Todd as one of the vocalists from the group Selah. When Angie went for her ultrasound at twenty weeks, she was told that the baby she was carrying would not be able to survive outside the womb.[1]

Any of you who have lost a child know a pain and a depth of grief that no one else knows, and it is only when you are finally in the presence of Christ and reunited with that little one that the gaping wound in your soul will be healed and whole. Yet I have watched in silent awe as women like Angie and others have learned to walk with this wound in a way that brings such glory to Christ.

> *Though Satan should buffet,*
> *though trials should come,*
> *Let this blest assurance control,*
> *That Christ has regarded my helpless estate,*
> *And hath shed His own blood for my soul.*[2]

ARE YOU THE ONE?

Have you ever been there? Have you ever found yourself in a place so ripe with pain and yet because of your commitment to Christ, you take the next step and the next because He is worth it? You and I live in the post-crucifixion and post-resurrection era, so by faith even the darkest nights hold the promise of home. But what about those who walked through nightmares before that Easter morning changed everything? What if you were the one sent to prepare the way for Messiah, but He wasn't what you expected or hoped for?

I think of the line that became famous from the movie *Field of Dreams*: "If you build it, they will come." In that context it was a baseball field that was being built with the assurance that if it was completed, the players would appear. But what if you had spent your life preparing the way for Christ, the Messiah, the one in whom every promise would be fulfilled, and when He arrived everything about Him seemed as wrong to you as a football player would on a baseball diamond? No one could have prepared the way more completely or with more passion than John the Baptist, but as Christ, who is the Shelter of all God's promises, appeared, John was shaken to his core.

There are few stories that move me as deeply in the New Testament as the story of John the Baptist. I feel a deep empathy for the kind of man he was. Even though I am a very "public" person, I am also a bit of a loner if given half a chance. Perhaps it is that side of John's life that I feel a great kinship with, but the part that moves me the most is how John died. I'm not even referring to his actual execution, which we know was a brutal, callous affair, but what was happening inside John's heart and mind right before he died.

John was a child of the wilderness and the desert. He was used to wide-open spaces, and now he was confined to a dungeon cell in the Castle of Machaerus built by Herod the Great. He had spent his whole life preparing for the moment when he would say, "Make straight the way for the Lord" (John 1:23), but now he sat in a dank dungeon cell, his life apparently in Herod's hands, and still the promised kingdom had not come. The prophet Isaiah told about the coming King who would liberate His people: "See, the Sovereign LORD comes with power, and his arm rules for him. See, his reward is with him, and his recompense accompanies him" (Isaiah 40:10).

As far as John could see, no kingdom had come, and he was left in this prison. Where was the promised liberation and victory? I can't imagine the disappointment and confusion and despair that must have settled on John. Jesus did not look to John like the Messiah. As the doubts began to plague his mind, he wondered if he had got it all wrong. What if he had given his life to prepare the way for the

Messiah and he identified the wrong person? So he asked two of his disciples to find Jesus and ask Him this question: "Are you the one who was to come, or should we expect someone else?" (Luke 7:20).

What must that have done to Christ's heart? How He must have wanted to tell John the Baptist what was going to happen. He must have longed to liberate John so that he could be there to witness the resurrection, but that was not in God's plan. So Jesus sent a message back to John with a strange statement at the end. He told them to tell John: "The blind receive sight, the lame walk, those who have leprosy are cured, the deaf hear, the dead are raised, and the good news is preached to the poor. Blessed is the man who does not fall away on account of me" (Luke 7:22–23).

In the first part of the statement, Jesus is quoting from Isaiah 61, but He did not quote the last part of the text, "to proclaim freedom for the captives and release from darkness for the prisoners" (Isaiah 61:1). There would be no liberation for John from this prison. In essence Jesus is saying, *I'm not coming for you, John. Others will taste of the liberty that I bring, but not you, not today.* Instead, Jesus says, "Blessed is the man who does not fall away on account of me."

How would that message have impacted John? Would it have been like rock salt rubbed into an open wound? *I am doing what Messiah is supposed to do, John, but not for you. You spent your whole life getting the stage set for Me, but I'm turning the light out on you. And I have just one question for you, John: do you still love Me?*

I can't read the story of this last brutal phase in John's life without weeping. He lived his whole life denying himself any sort of luxury or indulgence and had to place his head on a block with only one companion at his side, the executioner, without seeing what the road home through Christ was going to look like.

Christ's statement to John the Baptist begs a question that each one of us must answer at some point in our lives: will you love and serve a

God you do not always understand? It is crystal clear to me now that there are moments in life, heartaches that will make no sense this side of eternity.

Christ's statement to John the Baptist begs a question that each one of us must answer at some point in our lives: will you love and serve a God you do not always understand? Yes

Lord help make me willing

As C. G. Moore said:

> I know of no hours more trying to faith than those in which Jesus multiplies evidences of his power and does not use it. There is need of much grace when the messengers come back saying; "Yes, he has all the power, and is all that you have thought but he said not a word about taking you out of prison."[3]

That is the severe mercy for many believers who know that God could intervene, but for reasons known only to Him, He does not.

God is in control.

OUR PROMISE, OUR HOPE, OUR HOME

Paul expressed this reality and challenge so beautifully when he said in his first letter to the church in Corinth: "Now we see but a poor reflection as in a mirror; then we shall see face to face. Now I know in part; then I shall know fully, even as I am fully known" (1 Corinthians 13:12).

So I ask you with the deepest respect for the pain you have walked through, where is the dungeon in your life? Have you cried out or sent messages to Jesus asking Him to deliver some light to your dark night? Perhaps like John, you see Him do amazing things for other people, but no one has come to rescue you. Will you hear Him ask you as He asked John, *Do you still love Me? Will you tuck your life into the cleft of the rock and let Me be your shelter there? The wind will still howl and the night will still be dark, but I will never, ever leave you. That is My promise to you, and until you make it all the way home, I will be your home. I will be your Shelter.*

We are a people who do not live for this world. This is not our home. But until we finally see Jesus face-to-face, He has promised that He will never leave us. He has promised that He has gone ahead of us to prepare a place for us. What John could not see as he placed his head on the executioner's block was that the Shelter was almost complete.

CHRIST, THE SHELTER OF GOD'S PROMISES

When I began to think and pray through this book, I had one objective in mind that served as a plumb line as I wrote: *What are the promises of Christ that we can stake our lives on in the best and worst days?* Clearly, there are more promises than those I have included in this book. There are more than three thousand promises that take us from the first page of Genesis to the last words of the Revelation to John on Patmos. But I chose the ones that I saw, almost as foundation stones in a shelter, those that would take a lot of weight and weather the worst storms.

What are the promises of Christ that we can stake our lives on in the best and worst days?

As I worked through the material and read and reread the chapters, I began to see a picture emerge that initially I had not even considered. As the mist of deadlines and busyness began to clear, I saw something that was breathtakingly beautiful to me. I saw not only that all the promises of God are fulfilled in Christ to offer us shelter, but that He _is_ the Shelter. He _is_ the Cleft in the Rock. Christ's promise to us is not that He will give us shelter but that He will be our Shelter.

THE SHELTER IS COMPLETE

It started one night when a young girl, far away from home, gave birth in a place that offered little of the shelter a mother would want for a newborn baby. The canopy that night was heaven-sent as angels sang, "Glory to God in the highest, and on earth peace to men on whom his favor rests" (Luke 2:14). As Christ grew into manhood and began His ministry, His life was a divine show-and-tell of the heart of God, but no one understood. No one saw what He was building because that is human nature; we see what we want to see and often miss the greatest gift of all.

Some saw Him as a warrior because they wanted revenge against those who had oppressed them for so long. Some saw Him only as a miracle worker because they wanted life to be fixed, to make sense, and they wanted it now. Some saw Him as a man who spoke the truth in a world of half-truths, but few recognized that He is the Truth. With every act of love and kindness, every word of rebuke that cut through religious cloth, Jesus was laying the foundation that would lead the way to one radical statement that would change the world forever. When the final drop of blood fell from the cross onto the earth beneath and Jesus cried out, "It is finished," the Shelter was complete. Perhaps those who listened thought those words marked the end—how could they have known those words were the beginning of our liberty, our freedom? The Shelter is complete!

One day we will join John the Baptist and worship at the feet of Christ. Todd and Angie Smith will be there with their four children; you will be there, and so will I with every man, woman, and child who has put their trust and faith in Jesus Christ.

There are many things in this life I don't know, but I do know this: when we finally see Jesus, it will be worth it all. There will be many mothers in the crowd, but I hope I catch a glimpse of Mary. We left her at the foot of the cross, but that's not where she stayed.

When we finally see Jesus, it will be worth it all.

No, she was, even at the end, looking for her Jesus.

I wonder who told Mary first that Jesus was alive.

Was it John? I imagine him running as fast as he could (and he always makes a point in his gospel to make it clear that he was faster than Peter!) and throwing his arms around her fragile shoulders and telling her, "Jesus is alive!"

As she wiped the tears from her cheek, she knew that she would see her son again, but this time He would be her Savior. This time He would be the One to wipe the tears from her eyes.

And what beautiful eyes Mary shows us, for they had seen the Lord.

He is our Hope.

And He is our Home.

This is Christ's promise: to keep our hearts set on home with Him, with God, with the Holy Spirit. He has gone to prepare a place for us and left behind flagstones on which we can stand, a path for getting there. It is not simply that He has gone to prepare a place for us but that His death and resurrection have made it possible for us to be there with Him forever. That is the glorious gift of the gospel. Not only that, but Christ has promised that He will return and take us with Him to His home!

So until we see Him face-to-face, may you find shelter in His glorious promises.

NOTES

Chapter 1: Promises, Promises / *I Need Something to Hold On To*

1. Matthew Henry, *Matthew Henry's Concise Bible Commentary*, originally written from 1706 to 1721, public domain, exegesis of and commentary on Exodus 33:12–23.
2. From John Gill's *Exposition of the Bible* at BibleStudyTools.com on 2 Corinthians 1:20. Gill (1697–1771) preached in the same church as Charles Spurgeon, only one hundred years previously. His works are in the public domain, accessed online at the Bible Study Tools Web site (http://www.biblestudytools.com/commentaries /gills-exposition-of-the-bible/).

Chapter 2: Provision / *I Don't Have Enough*

1. Neal Jeffrey, *If I Can, Y-Y-You Can!* (Dallas, TX: Samson, 2009), 107.
2. Dr. Ralph F. Wilson, "Thanksgiving and the Pilgrims: Don't Ask the Blessing, Offer One," online article at the Joyful Heart Renewal Ministries Web site, http://www.joyfulheart.com/thanksgiving /offer-blessing.htm.

Chapter 3: Peace / *I'm Afraid and Feel Alone*

1. Words and music by Bob Bennett, "Man of the Tombs" © 1989 Matters of the Heart Music (ASCAP), www.bobbennett.com. Used with permission of the publisher and the author.

2. Ibid.
3. Ibid.

Chapter 4: Confidence / *I Can't See God's Plan in This Pain*

1. A. W. Tozer, *We Travel an Appointed Way* (Camp Hill, PA: Christian Publications, 1988), 3.
2. Sarah Young, *Jesus Calling* (Brentwood, TN: Integrity, 2004), 134.
3. Robert J. Morgan, *The Promise* (Nashville, TN: B & H, 2008), 91.
4. Edwin and Lillian Harvey and E. Hey, *They Knew Their God*, vol. 1 (Harvey and Tait Publishers, 1980; Old Tract Path Society, 1996), about Samuel Logan Brendle (1860–1936), "Soldier and Servant."

Chapter 5: Love / *I Don't Believe That Anyone Could Really Love Me*

1. There is a reference to "daughter" in Luke 23:28, when Jesus turns to a crowd of women mourners who are following Him up the Via Dolorosa, where He will be crucified, and says, "Daughters of Jerusalem, do not weep for me; weep for yourselves and for your children." But the hemorrhaging woman was the only woman we are told about whom Jesus looked full in the face and called "daughter."

Chapter 6: Grace / *I Have Failed*

1. According to the Web site Marriage 101, the divorce rate in America for a first marriage is 41 percent; for a second marriage it is 60 percent. "Divorce Rates in America," http://marriage101.org/divorce-rates-in-america/.
2. Raymond E. Marley, "Is It the Home of Peter? Miraculous Discoveries in the 'City of Miracles,'" *Jerusalem Christian Review* 9, Internet ed., issue 1; available at http://www.leaderu.com/theology/isithome.html.

Chapter 7: Hope / *I'm Broken*

1. Randy Elrod as quoted on his blog on June 15, 2010 (www.randyelrod.com), in a post titled "The Lie About Sexual Inequality."
2. Helen Roseveare, *Give Me This Mountain* (Gleanies House, Fearn, Ross-shire, Scotland: Christian Focus, 2006, 1966), 86.
3. Tonya Stoneman, "Can You Thank Me for This?" Online at www.suffering.net/thank.htm.
4. William McDonald, *The Believer's Bible* commentary (Nashville, TN: Thomas Nelson, 1995), commentary on Luke 7:37–38, p. 1395.

Chapter 8: Strength / *I Feel Things Are Crashing Around Me*

1. Joni Eareckson Tada, "Joy Hard Won," *Decision*, March 2000, 12.
2. John Keats, letter to Benjamin Bailey, May 25, 1918, available at http://englishhistory.net/keats/letters/bailey2125May1818.html.

Chapter 9: More / *I Know There's Something Better*

1. *The New Bible Dictionary* (Leicester, England: IVP, 1962), s.v. "blessed."
2. C. S. Lewis, *The Weight of Glory* (New York: HarperCollins, 2001), 26.
3. *The Word Biblical Commentary* identifies this passage as a pericope, as does *The Expositors Bible Commentary*.
4. William Barclay, *The Gospel of St. Matthew*, vol. 1 (Louisville, KY: Westminster John Knox Press, rev. ed. 1975), 271.

Chapter 10: Home / *I Have a Future*

1. Angie Smith, *I Will Carry You: The Sacred Dance of Grief and Joy* (Nashville: B&H, 2010).
2. "It Is Well with My Soul," lyrics by Horatio G. Spafford. Public domain.
3. C. G. Moore as quoted by W. H. Griffith Thomas, *Outline Studies in the Book of Luke*, (Grand Rapids: Kregel, 1998), 129.

BIBLE STUDY

CHAPTER 1: PROMISES, PROMISES

Discover

Read 2 Corinthians 1:20 and Exodus 33; then answer the following questions:

1. How do you see that God's promises have been fulfilled in the person of Christ?

2. Moses wanted to *know* that his identity was in God and not in himself (Exodus 33:15–16). How do you know that your identity is in Christ? *Gods presence with me*

3. Even though God's people were faithless, He was willing to have compassion on them (v. 19). Why? *mercy compassion*

4. How did God provide shelter for the Israelites? How is He your Shelter?

Believe

5. We all have different stories to tell, and many of us will approach the idea of God's promises from unique perspectives. So, what comes to mind when you think of the promises of God?

6. In Exodus 33, Moses pleads with God to remember His promises. What were those promises, and how did God remember them? (page 7)

7. We're promised that God keeps us in His hand. Do you feel "kept in Christ"? When do you feel that most strongly (e.g., during times of crisis, when you've spent time in His Word, etc.)?

8. Why would God want to keep His promises to us when we mess up so badly, so often? *love*

Live

9. Because we live in a world where we are the recipients of many promises that will never be kept, is it difficult for you to grasp that God's promises will never be broken? Why? *Trust*

10. "God's promises are not about us but about Him" (page 14). Explain, in your own words, what this means. Have you experienced this personally? *He can't help Himself*

11. How do you bring your focus back to the promises of God when life has given you difficult detours, such as the loss of a family member, an illness, or other periods of sadness? *That's all we have*

MEMORIZE THIS WEEK: "For no matter how many promises God has made, they are 'Yes' in Christ. And so through him the 'Amen' is spoken by us to the glory of God." (2 Corinthians 1:20)

CHAPTER 2: PROVISION

Discover

Read Mark 6; then answer the following questions:

1. Why did Jesus instruct His disciples not to pack supplies and provisions for their mission? Does this seem strange to you? How would you have responded in this situation?

2. What did Jesus expect for (and from) the disciples?

3. The disciples reported to Christ all the work they'd done, and He said to them, "Come with me by yourselves to a quiet place and get some rest" (vv. 30–31). What do you imagine they talked about while they rested? What "rest" has Christ offered you in your daily routine?

Believe

4. When you take an honest assessment of your life today, what needs do you have? Do you fear God won't provide in those areas?

5. Do you believe that when you rest in Jesus, truly anything is possible? What are the "impossible" things in your life today that you want God to make possible?

Live

6. God promises to provide for whatever mission He's called us on. What daunting mission has God assigned to you? Are you up for the task?

7. There are times when words don't help and our friends can't touch the grief we feel; we can only turn to Jesus. How has He met your needs today? This week? This year?

8. Jesus offers us the opportunity to run away with Him, escape from the stresses of life, and relax. Have you ever taken Him up on this invitation?

9. Where do you go to refuel when you're exhausted? Where does God want you to go? What practical thing will you do this week to turn to God for your rest?

MEMORIZE THIS WEEK: "And my God will meet all your needs according to his glorious riches in Christ Jesus." (Philippians 4:19)

CHAPTER 3: PEACE

Discover

Read Mark 4:35–5:13; then answer the following questions:

1. Jesus and His disciples were making an uncomfortable journey to an unpleasant place (read more on pages 46–47). Why did they make this effort? *Jesus was on a mission*

2. When Christ speaks to the storms inside and outside a person's heart, both obey. What does this mean for you? *Peace assurance*

3. How is the authority of Jesus, seen in this story in dramatic fashion, a source of comfort to His followers?

Believe

4. The Greek word for "peace" is *eirene*, which means "a state of untroubled, undisturbed well-being." How would you define peace, based on your life experiences? *Calmness*

5. Have you ever found yourself tormented by the choices you're making in life, or in turmoil over a sense of self-hatred that you feel? How can you move from that place to a place of peace in Christ? *Prayer Believe*

6. Do you long for your life to tell a different story from the one you're living? If so, what would that story be?

7. What would you say to the Gadarene demoniac or to the homeless man in the London park if you had the opportunity to meet one of them? How would you communicate God's love to them? *listen, care, love them*

Live

8. Have you ever experienced the waves crashing over the boat that is your life, fearing you'll drown in the storm that surrounds you? What has brought you to that place?

9. In what ways did Jesus calm the seas for you?

194

10. What are the wounds you have been living with in your life? Are you willing to invite God in to heal them?

MEMORIZE THIS WEEK: "Peace I leave with you; my peace I give you." (John 14:27)

CHAPTER 4: CONFIDENCE

Discover

Read 2 Kings 17:34–40 (about the Samaritans) and John 4:1–26; then answer the following questions:

1. Why were the Samaritans so repulsive to the Jews? (See pages 60–61 for more.)
2. In what ways did Jesus' conversation with the Samaritan woman emphasize the idea that His gift of salvation is a *free* gift?
3. How do we see the truth of Romans 8:28 ("all things God works for the good of those who love him") in the Samaritan woman's story? What was her legacy?

Believe

4. God promises that He will use all things for good for those who love Him. Do you believe that's true for your life? Take some time to imagine how that might happen.
5. Why did the Jews hate the Samaritans so deeply? Have you ever witnessed or experienced that kind of resentment?
6. What do you believe will make you happy in this life? What does Scripture promise will make us happy?
7. Jesus doesn't berate the Samaritan woman for her many dalliances with men; instead, He offers her the only relationship that will ever satisfy—one with Himself. How does the intimacy of Jesus' compassion and the generosity of His gift of salvation impact you?

Live

8. In what areas of your life—your looks, your wealth, your family, etc.—have you felt alone or isolated, even ashamed, as though you didn't measure up?

9. How might God use the pain in your life to bring you closer to Him? Has that happened in your experience?

10. Do you consider the Holy Spirit to be your prayer partner? How might viewing Him in this way change your prayer life? your perspective on the issues you struggle with regularly?

MEMORIZE THIS WEEK: "And we know that in all things God works for the good of those who love him, who have been called according to his purpose." (Romans 8:28)

CHAPTER 5: LOVE

*power out him
gone from*

Discover

Read Mark 5:24–34; then answer the following questions:

out of options desperate unbelievable

1. How did Jesus know the woman had touched Him? What is the significance of His power going out to her?

2. What mental anguish do you imagine the woman was living with? Why was she willing to take the risk to touch Jesus?

3. How do you think the woman felt, knowing that she'd been healed immediately? Do you think this was a story she told for the rest of her life?

Believe

4. Many people feel ostracized by Christian communities. Has God convicted you to reach out the hand of love toward any specific group that may be feeling rejected by the church?

5. What problem or issue are you facing in your life today? This week? This year? Look up a promise from God's Word that addresses it (use a concordance or topical index as a reference), and then read over that verse every day as a reminder of God's love and salvation.

6. Jesus never gives us what *we think* we need, instead He gives us what *He knows* we need. Have you seen this to be true in your life?

Live

7. The woman who was hemorrhaging, in Mark's gospel, took a tremendous risk to reach out and touch Jesus' robe. She was desperate for an answer to her problems; she'd risk everything for hope. Have you ever felt that way?

8. When have you reached out for hope and clung to it like a lifeline? What was it that restored your hope in Christ? *peace*

9. How has love transformed your life?

10. Have you ever told Jesus the whole truth about your life? Take some time to journal your testimony—the story of your life seen through the filter of Jesus pursuing you to be His child. Then pray, thanking Jesus for His gift of redemption.

MEMORIZE THIS WEEK: "For I am convinced that neither death nor life, neither angels nor demons, neither the present nor the future, nor any powers, neither height nor depth, nor anything else in all creation, will be able to separate us from the love of God that is in Christ Jesus our Lord." (Romans 8:38–39)

CHAPTER 6: GRACE

Discover

Read Luke 15:11–32; then answer the following questions:

1. Make a list of all the offensive or shocking elements that are found in this story, such as the son demanding his inheritance or the son living among unclean pigs. Why did Jesus go to this extreme to show such a rebellious boy?
2. What do we learn about God's grace in this story?
3. Close your eyes and imagine the scene, with yourself as that rebellious son and God the Father running down the path to embrace you in His arms. How does this make you feel? Does it motivate you in any way?

Believe *Who he is, not how we act*

4. Do you, deep down, believe that God loves all of us equally; or do you think He actually likes people more when they have dedicated their lives to service and sacrifice?
5. The only place where we can experience unconditional love is at the heart of God. That divine love is called *grace*. When you hear the word "grace," what comes to mind?
6. When you hear the story of the prodigal son, with whom do you most identify? Why? Do you believe that aspect of your personal character can receive grace?
7. Why does God hide from us some of the mysteries of the faith? How do these mysteries impact your spiritual life?

Live

8. God has the kind of strength that fills in all our weaknesses. Think back to a time when God was the strength you needed. List the ways He provided for you in your need. *peace*
9. How have you experienced God's "unprecedented, outrageous, overwhelming" love?
10. What will it take for you to recognize your need for God's lavish, unmerited grace in your life?

MEMORIZE THIS WEEK: "My grace is sufficient for you, for my power is made perfect in weakness." (2 Corinthians 12:9)

CHAPTER 7: HOPE

Discover
Read Luke 8:1–3, and then answer the following questions:

1. What was the source of Mary Magdalene's pain before she met Jesus? *demons*
2. How did her encounter with Him change her life forever? Feel free to imagine what happened the day Jesus rescued her. *more*
3. Has "heaven invaded your hell"? What happened, and how are you different?

Believe

4. Think of your dreams for your life. Imagine the possibilities and consider your expectations. How do God's promises fit into that vision?
5. Review the Scriptures mentioned in this chapter and think of other examples you know from your own Bible study—when have people in the Bible struggled, and how did God provide for them?
6. In what ways did Mary Magdalene struggle to grasp God's promises? How can you learn from her?
7. God promises He will never, *ever*, leave us. Do you, deep down, truly believe that?

Live

8. Do you ever feel tempted to "enhance" God's promises, as if you're His personal PR agent?

9. What painful and lonely situations have you had to walk through in life? Did you feel on your own? Or did you sense God supporting you?

10. In this chapter we read that God is Light, Love, Grace, a Gift, a Cleft for us to hide in. In your own words, what is Christ to you?

MEMORIZE THIS WEEK: "God has said, 'Never will I leave you; never will I forsake you.' So we say with confidence, 'The Lord is my helper; I will not be afraid.'" (Hebrews 13:5–6)

CHAPTER 8: STRENGTH

Discover

Read John 13:1–17; then answer the following questions:

1. Verse 3 from this passage shows us the "why" for Jesus' behavior that night. What was His motivation, and what does it mean for *you*?

2. Peter's enthusiastic all-in response is typical for him. Do you respond this way, or are you more cautious? Do you think there's a right or wrong to this?

3. How does this scene show us the point of Jesus' promises to us (see page 143 for more)?

Believe

4. In what ways have you been living a "careful life"? Have you been holding back on who God designed you to be? Why?

5. God promised Isaiah, "I will give you hidden treasures, riches stored in secret places, so that you may know that I am the LORD, the God of Israel, who summons you by name" (Isaiah 45:3). What treasures have you discovered in the darkness of your journey?

6. How can we know, or how can we remind ourselves, that God is there upholding us even when the night is black and the pain is crowding the life out of us? What, specifically, can you do to hold on to the hope of God's light when all you see is blackness?

7. Jesus chose to spend His final hours on earth in a place of weakness and humility—washing His disciples' feet. Why? How did He "overcome the world" in this moment?

Live

8. We've all had struggles in this life, some more threatening than others. Have you ever experienced the emotion John Keats described this way: "I am in that temper that if I were under water I would scarcely kick to come to the top"? Have you ever wanted to give up? What has kept you going?

9. Even though Jesus knew the pain He'd have to face on the cross, He took time to stop and pray for His friends. What pain are your friends and family suffering right now? None of us escapes unscathed, so if you're not aware of their struggles, dig deeper into those relationships this week and find out what's hurting those you love. Then step into the journey by praying for and loving them.

10. Jesus' promise is, "Take heart! I have overcome the world." How does this change your perspective today?

MEMORIZE THIS WEEK: "In this world you will have trouble. But take heart! I have overcome the world." (John 16:33)

CHAPTER 9: MORE

Discover

Read Matthew 5:17–20; then answer the following questions:

1. Why was observance of the law so important to the Jewish people of Jesus' day?
2. What does it mean that Jesus came "to fulfill the law"?
3. Do you believe you live by the law or by God's grace? Why?

Believe

4. What have you been dreaming of obtaining lately—new paint in the living room, a new dining room table, a fashionable outfit for an important event, a nicer house? Write down your list of "I wants" in a journal or on a separate piece of paper. Now write down how long you think those things will satisfy you before you want to replace them.
5. What do you think Jesus really meant when He told us, "Ask, and it will be given to you" (Matthew 7:7)? How does He satisfy your desires?
6. On page 153, the different layers of meaning that the word *blessed* contains are discussed. How would you define this word? Why is it a significant choice for starting the Sermon on the Mount?
7. Why were the religious leaders so incensed—furious even—with Jesus for His Sermon on the Mount message?

Live

8. Why is life so much more complicated and stressful when we focus on the rules? What should we focus on?
9. Read through the Sermon on the Mount (Matthew 5 to 7) with fresh eyes. What deep habits or expectations of yours did Jesus turn upside down in this passage of Scripture?
10. Think back to your list of items from Question 4. What is it you're *really* seeking in life? How do God's promises fulfill these desires?

MEMORIZE THIS WEEK: "Ask and it will be given to you; seek and you will find; knock and the door will be opened to you. For everyone who asks receives; he who seeks finds; and to him who knocks, the door will be opened." (Matthew 7:7–8)

CHAPTER 10: HOME

Discover

Read John 14:2–3 and John 19:16–27; then answer the following questions:

1. What do you think Mary thought as she watched Jesus grow into an adult? Do you think she feared she'd misunderstood everything when she watched Him being crucified?
2. How are these two passages of Scripture connected? What meaning do they hold for you?
3. How is Jesus' promise to provide for you, to be your shelter, central to what you believe?

Believe

4. What fears, joys, and sadness did Mary experience as the mother of the Son of God, especially as she watched him grow into a man?
5. What stirs your soul when you read the story of Mary, mother of Jesus?
6. This chapter talks about the doubts all those who knew Jesus must have felt. What doubts have you experienced? Has Jesus answered them yet?

Live

7. When Mary is told of her daunting task—bearing the Son of God—she responds with confident humility, "I am the Lord's servant . . . May it be to me as you have said." (Luke 1:38). Have you been as willing to accept the will of God when you've encountered challenges in your life?

8. Have you ever found yourself in a place ripe with pain, yet because of your commitment to Christ, you're willing to take the next step in faith? What happened?

9. To what extent are you willing to love and serve a God you do not always understand? How far are you willing to go to serve Him?

10. When John realized that Jesus was alive, he ran as fast as he could to Mary to tell her that she would see her Son again and, this time, He would be her Savior. Who gave you this wonderful message? Have you shared it with anyone else?

MEMORIZE THIS WEEK: "In my Father's house are many rooms; if it were not so, I would have told you. I am going there to prepare a place for you." (John 14:2)

ABOUT THE AUTHOR

Sheila Walsh is a communicator, Bible teacher, and best-selling author with more than four million books sold. A featured speaker with Women of Faith, Sheila has reached more than three and a half million women by artistically combining honesty, vulnerability, and humor with God's Word.

Author of the best-selling memoir *Honestly* and the Gold Medallion nominee for *The Heartache No One Sees*, Sheila's latest release, *The Shelter of God's Promises*, is a companion to a twelve-week Bible study. She released her first novel, *Angel Song*, and has written several children's books, including *Gigi, God's Little Princess*, which has a companion video series that has won the National Retailer's Choice Award twice and is the most popular Christian brand for young girls in the United States.

Sheila cohosted *The 700 Club* and her own show, *Heart to Heart with Sheila Walsh*. She is currently completing her master's in theology and lives in Dallas, Texas, with her husband, Barry, son, Christian, and two little dogs, Belle and Tink.

Visit her Web site at www.sheilawalsh.com.
Facebook: www.facebook.com/sheilawalshconnects
Twitter: @sheilawalsh / www.twitter.com/sheilawalsh

ALSO AVAILABLE:
THE SHELTER OF GOD'S PROMISES
DVD-BASED BIBLE STUDY
& PARTICIPANT'S GUIDE

Join Sheila Walsh for biblical teaching and powerful personal testimony that will help you learn about God's promises to us, what His promises mean, and how they provide the foundation for daily confidence, joy, & hope. The DVD-Based Study features include: Ten, 25 to 30-minute sessions and bonus resources for promoting your Bible study or small group series.

THOMAS NELSON
Since 1798

For other products and live events,
visit us at: thomasnelson.com

DVD-BASED BIBLE STUDY

SHEILA WALSH

THE
SHELTER
OF
GOD'S PROMISES

PARTICIPANT'S GUIDE

SHEILA WALSH
WITH TRACEY D. LAWRENCE

THE
SHELTER
OF
GOD'S PROMISES